A Scientific Approach to Ethics

Maxim Storchevoy

A Scientific Approach to Ethics

Developing Greater Respect for Ethics in Business and Society

Maxim Storchevoy
Graduate School of Management
St. Petersburg University

National Research University Higher School of Economics
St. Petersburg, Russia

ISBN 978-3-319-69112-1   ISBN 978-3-319-69113-8   (eBook)
https://doi.org/10.1007/978-3-319-69113-8

Library of Congress Control Number: 2017960754

Cover illustration: Pattern adapted from an Indian cotton print produced in the 19th century

Printed on acid-free paper

This Palgrave Macmillan imprint is published by Springer Nature
The registered company is Springer International Publishing AG
The registered company address is: Gewerbestrasse 11, 6330 Cham, Switzerland

PREFACE

From the dawn of philosophy, the question concerning the summum bonum, or, what is the same thing, concerning the foundation of morality, has been accounted the main problem in speculative thought, has occupied the most gifted intellects, and divided them into sects and schools, carrying on a vigorous warfare against one another. And after more than two thousand years the same discussions continue, philosophers are still ranged under the same contending banners, and neither thinkers nor mankind at large seem nearer to being unanimous on the subject, than when the youth Socrates listened to the old Protagoras, and asserted (if Plato's dialogue be grounded on a real conversation) the theory of utilitarianism against the popular morality of the so-called sophist. (Mill, Utilitarianism, chapter 1, paragraph 1)

These words of John Stuart Mill may be repeated today. The moral philosophy landscape is constituted by an even higher diversity of approaches and "the same contending banners" are fluttering over the battlefields. Sure, diversity and academic creativity are good, but real progress in any discipline is achieved when these two virtues are complemented with the discipline of the highest intellectual rigor aimed at comparing various approaches and choosing the most valid ones. In other words diversity and creativity should be combined with scientific method. Otherwise moral philosophy will continue to develop as literature or art. Of course, ethics as literature or art is a legitimate genre with its own entertaining or enlightening purposes, but what about ethics as a science?

This book grew out of deep dissatisfaction with methodological weakness in normative ethics which leads to uncertain conclusions and eventually a lack of respect from students and other people. Is it possible to change this situation? Can we apply to ethics the same scientific method which made productive and successful disciplines such as physics, biology, or economics?

I suggest that this is possible. We can render normative ethics as a science with clear definitions, strict logic, possibility of empirical verification, and accurate collection of empirical data. This scientific ethics may lead to clear falsifiable propositions which may win unanimous support from scholars and trust from society.

It is interesting that almost all elements of scientific ethics appeared in the writings of the major philosophers from the seventeenth to the nineteenth centuries (definition of good, rational choice, social contract, the role of knowledge and feelings, etc.) and, theoretically, normative ethics could develop into a science in the early twentieth century (e.g. as was the case with economics). However, this did not happen. This could be attributed to the influence of Moore, the linguistic turn, or the absence of several important tools like collective choice theory or veil of ignorance. In any case it seems to be a fundamental and sad mistake that normative ethics was not developed as a science in the twentieth century.

The purpose of this book is to prove that scientific ethics is possible. Although it may sound radical, it requires not a revolution but just a last step in assembling together the tools and concepts of various traditions according scientific standards. Moreover, this method will eventually lead to similar answers within these traditions, but these answers may now be claimed to be a proved scientific knowledge.

I do not claim that this book provides a complete resolution of all methodological issues. I want to prove only that we should accept scientific methods in normative ethics. The best variants to apply this method should be discussed further and may be different from what is suggested in this text.

The book is organized as follows: In Chap. 1 we talk about the lack of respect for moral philosophy in our society (and especially from students) and discuss the general methodological structure of ethics. In Chap. 2 we suggest a possible scientific approach to normative ethics based on individual rational choice (which serves as a foundation in other social sciences). In Chap. 3 we describe the new evolutionary model of man explaining the role of emotions, culture, and reason in rational choice,

which is important for normative ethics. In Chap. 4 we discuss the historical development of moral philosophy before the twentieth century and
trace the evolution of its attitude to a scientific approach and the appearance of all theoretical elements which may be necessary in scientific ethics.
Chapter 5 examines the position of Moore and meta-ethics which were so
influential for moral philosophy in the twentieth century. In Chap. 6 we
discuss the development of contractarianism and rational choice approaches
which came the closest to a scientific approach to ethics. In Chap. 7 we
discuss several other approaches (emotivism, intuitionism, prescriptivism,
virtue ethics) and their scientific status.

This book does not claim to be a complete analysis of the relevant literature. The choice of some authors may even seem arbitrary. However,
this is only a result of limitation of time and space. I focused mainly on
books as a more mature philosophical position of their authors, but surely
there are also hundreds of academic publications that might be also interesting to analyze from this perspective. This task requires a larger text and
will be pursued in the future.

St. Petersburg, Russia   Maxim Storchevoy

CONTENTS

LIST OF FIGURES

LIST OF TABLES

CHAPTER 1

Why Science? What Science?

Abstract Is it possible to build ethics like a science? Many ordinary people think that this is impossible because there are too many subjective opinions and disagreements. Many scholars think that this is not necessary and some of them emphasize that there is no true science at all. However, is it so? Can the "impossible" or "unnecessary" theses, be proved? This chapter suggests the opposite. We can and should rebuild ethics as a science. First, it will help to significantly increase its analytical quality and achieve better theoretical progress. Second, it will upgrade the weak status of this discipline in society and business.

Keywords • Business ethics • Ethics • Science • Truth • Verification

Is ethics a science? Can it be a science? Should it be a science? There are no clear and comprehensive answers for these questions. Obviously, ethics is a well-established discipline in the global academic community: there are several peer-reviewed journals, popular world-wide conferences, etc. And while it has many attributes of a science, it is not developed like a science. It seems that moral philosophers have an implicit consensus that this is impossible or unnecessary. Is this so? The book will try to discuss this problem in detail and to suggest some steps for improvement.

© The Author(s) 2018   1
M. Storchevoy, *A Scientific Approach to Ethics*,
https://doi.org/10.1007/978-3-319-69113-8_1

THE PROBLEM

Can ethics be a science? Many philosophers would possibly answer "no" and some would add "why it should be?" However, there is at least one serious practical problem created by this state of mind—*lack of respect in society for the discipline.*

I refer to my experience of teaching business ethics and moral reasoning for managers. First, it is easy to observe an obvious *lack of respect for ethics from students.* If we look into business ethics textbooks, we will find a diversity of approaches to present normative theories, but not an academic rigor common for textbooks in physics or economics. As a result, a common attitude of students attending a business ethics course is that "this is entertaining but not serious" or even worse "it is a waste of time." I conducted several surveys to observe students' attitude to business ethics as a discipline. First, the students were exposed to all main approaches (golden rule, divine command, virtues ethics, natural law, intuitionism, Utilitarianism, Kant, Rawls, corporate social responsibility, stakeholder theory) and were asked to discuss their weak and strong sides. After this the students were asked to answer the question "Can moral theory be a science?" This is a sample of typical responses.

- "We cannot call moral theory a science because science has to be based on objective knowledge and we cannot conclude that moral theory is objective because it is very dubious notion."
- "Moral theory is based on some perceptions which a hard to measure and compare. Morality is very subjective."
- "In order to check moral theory for falsifiability we may take as example utilitarianism, which says that an action may be called "right" if it maximizes good consequences. It is rather hard to falsify this statement because the criteria of goodness is not objective, it is our sense and there is no certain way to measure good or bad consequences."
- "Moral theory is subjective and is not measurable by any numbers. This is the main hurdle to deal with it as a science."
- "Moral theory cannot be a science because: (1) no objective data, (2) no measurement of morality, (3) no criteria to refer facts to theories, (4) an empirical check is impossible, (5) no reproducible results."
- "Moral theory cannot be referred to as general truth as it differs within different centuries and societies."

- "Moral theory is closely interconnected with religion which contradicts science."
- "Moral norms are always relative and subjective because there is no clear definition of what is moral. It is not universal because it varies from society to society, from place to place, etc."
- "Scientific theories are objective, i.e. they exist regardless of individual perception. Law of gravity remains unchanged in Ghana, Russia or China. It is possible to verify it by observation and experiment. Moral theory does not meet this requirement."
- "Everything in science should be proved to be considered as a truth but this is impossible in moral theory."
- "The basis of considering things or actions in moral theory is subjective and unstable, because it is based on feelings, senses and emotions."
- "Science has some attributes: it is systematic, well-organized knowledge in the forms of explanations and predictions. Moral theory does not actually respond to any of these features. It is too flexible, non-systematic, its predictions are hazy."
- "It is not known whether morality is a national variable. If it depends on a particular society, each society should have its own theory."

Maybe this lack of respect was a result of my poor teaching skills? Or improper pedagogy? This is rarely so. First, my students are usually quite excited by business ethics classes, so this is not a "boring professor" problem. Second, in this experiment I deliberately followed a standard approach of presenting alternative theories and discussing them like the authors of many business ethics textbooks do, so the outcome of such a survey in many other business schools would not be very different.[1] A similar account on the cynical or skeptical attitude of students is provided in the book on ethics in economics (Hausman et al. 2016).[2]

The second and no less important problem is *lack of respect from the business community*. On the one hand, many professionals graduate from a handful of business schools, so this skeptical attitude is formed at the university bench. On the other hand, in recurring situations of ethical controversies the business community almost never hears the distinctive voice of a business ethics specialist who may confidentially resolve an issue. However, such a "scientific voice" is normally heard in other areas of human activity, e.g. professional opinion of physicists may resolve concern about global warming, the professional opinion of medical researchers may resolve concern about new disease treatment, etc. Normally, people have respect for science and follow recommendations of science in their ordinary lives. When geneticists say that some disease has genetic origins or cholesterol is not dangerous, we trust them because we know that *this is science*. However, when was the last time we have heard that business ethicists discovered some new moral truth?

Holland and Albrecht (2013) asked 211 scholars with expertise in business ethics to identify the three most important issues that business ethics academia will face in the near future. The first two were issues relating to *business ethics education* and the *credibility of business ethics*. By credibility they understood acceptance, legitimacy, respect, and recognition among students, academia, benefactors, and practitioners. Typical examples of responses were: "The scornful attitude of business school faculty: ethics is not academically legitimate or rigorous," and "Taken seriously by other colleagues."

Who is responsible for this lack of authority? My guess is that the academic community in the business ethics domain, and in moral philosophy in general, traditionally supports pluralism and freedom of opinions (which is obviously a good thing!), but at the same time does not pay enough attention to accuracy, logical rigor, and verification which are so important in other scientific domains (e.g. economics, physics, or medicine). The entry "Problems of moral philosophy" in *The Oxford Companion to Philosophy* tells us that "the major problem of current and traditional moral philosophy, then, is coming up with a rationally defensible theory of right and wrong action" (Honderich 2005, pp. 626–627). There are five approaches (Utilitarianism, Kantianism, contractualism, intuitivism, virtue ethics) but "no generally accepted solutions" to disagreement between them.[3]

This attitude is manifested in *business ethics textbooks* which demonstrate a rich diversity of approaches and colorful cases, but lack academic rigor. They present various frameworks (Utilitarianism, Deontology, virtue ethics, etc.) without trying to reduce them to a common denominator.[4]

A similar situation is observed in teaching social responsibility to engineers and natural scientists (Zandvoort et al. 2013). There are several evidences that ethics is excluded from technical education because of its non-scientific nature:

> most engineering courses are traditionally taught in a fashion which is highly divorced from real engineering practice (Ozaktas 2011);

Because (sustainable development) is an ambiguous concept, it is a challenge especially to engineers and engineering education, as they have traditionally focused on teaching 'absolute facts' (Takala and Korhonen-Yrjänheikki 2011);

[We can explain] the lack of ethical elements in university science education by identifying the logic underlying science curricula: they are about learning to solve scientific puzzles that have exactly one answer. Ethical problems, however, are contextual and complex and seldom have only one solution. This explains why ethical elements are excluded from mainstream university science programs: they do not fit in (Børsen et al. 2013);

Ethics teaching in engineering can be problematic because of student perceptions of its subjective, ambiguous and philosophical content. (Alpay 2011)

This multi-confessionality with lack of criticism may be good in religion or in art but it is hardly a good thing in science. Normally, in other sciences like physics or mathematics, when two alternative theories become the subject of deep discussion, the scholars usually aim at resolving the conflict through logical proof or empirical verification, but there is no such practice in ethics. Moral philosophers in much less degree compete for logical or empirical supremacy, seek conceptual parsimony, or claim truth than their colleagues in other disciplines. How then can moral philosophers persuade students and other people that ethical theory can tell undeniable moral truth if they cannot persuade each other?

I suggest that we can persuade each other and the society if we develop and present *a scientific approach* to moral philosophy and business ethics—an approach that will leave no room for skepticism and lack of respect.

WHAT SCIENCE?

What science is the closest relative to ethics? It seems that a scientific ethics should belong to social sciences, because it is about human behavior and human relationships. Therefore, its closest relatives should be psychology, sociology, economics, and political science. Moreover, there should be substantial overlapping of these disciplines with scientific ethics because all of them historically developed some concepts and ideas which essentially should belong to moral theory (choice, norms, values, conflict, etc.).

If ethics is a social science then its progress probably depends even more on good methodology than if it were a natural science because social phenomena have a much more complex and less deterministic nature. The history of social science shows that progress in any of them is very problematic without a clear understanding of its research task, corresponding methodology, and clear criteria for evaluating, criticizing, and developing the contributions of colleagues. We can refer to the experience of one of the most successful social sciences in the twentieth century—economics. It achieved progress after developing a unifying neo-classical methodology and adopting scientific methods in the early twentieth century. Since then any theoretical claim in economics must be logically proved and empirically verified. As a result the field of economics achieved significant progress. In 1960s its scientific status was recognized by the Nobel Prize committee by establishing a special reward. An important factor of this success was a clear distinction for positive economics, normative economics, and economic policy which was adopted in the 1920s–1930s. Interestingly, that huge success was achieved mostly in positive economics and economic policy, but normative economics was mostly underdeveloped because it lacked a good foundation.

Distinction between normative and positive analysis has existed in ethics for a long time, but it seems that philosophers do not always accurately follow it. Moral philosophy was, for a long time, understood as "practical philosophy" because it told people how they should live. To establish a clear methodological principle for ethics as a science we need to distinguish three separate branches of ethics: normative, positive, and practical.

Normative ethics should answer the question "what is good" and "what is right." It may use the achievements of positive sciences as data for analysis but its main research question should be normative and it should have its own methodology (a scientific variant of this methodology will be discussed in the next chapter).

Positive ethics should answer the question "how people make ethical choices in reality." It should be descriptive and explanatory, but it need not have its own methodology. It can only borrow methods from other social disciplines (economics, sociology, psychology) and serve only as a general contractor who defines the research question and compiles findings. Its main suppliers will be: (1) economic methodology, can explain how rational actors make their choices in various situations, (2) sociology, can describe real practices and institutions that exist in real communities, and (3) psychology, can study cognitive and emotional processes.

Practical ethics should answer two questions. The first question is asked by any *person*: "How do I want to live my life?" Normative ethics could provide some practical rules on how to make right decisions and cope with difficult moral issues. A special problem is how to make oneself comply with moral norms, and here some tips and methods may be suggested by psychologists. Many historical ethical approaches may be related to this genre (e.g. the Ten Commandments were a practical code of individual ethics, Stoics taught how to achieve eudaimonic life by psychological practices). The second question is asked by a *regulator* (church, manager, government): "How to make people behave according to moral norms?" Normative ethics defines "ought," and positive ethics, "is," and the regulator should bring the latter to the former. Here practical ethics may borrow tools from management, education theory, economics, and other disciplines.

In this book we will focus mostly on the scientific methodology of normative ethics because it seems to be the most disputable problem that prevents progress in general as well as applied normative ethics (e.g. business ethics).

NOTES

1. Compare an evidence from about 60 years ago: "Students of ethics are apt to be disappointed to find that, although the subject has been studied for over two thousand years, it does not seem to have produced any established system of truths comparable to those of mathematics and the natural sciences. Why is Aristotle's Ethics still worth reading, while his Physics is of interest only to scholars and historians?" (Nowell-Smith 1952, p. 15).
2. Moral questions and moral reasoning can be difficult to understand, and we have found that students often hold very skeptical or even cynical views. One hears claims such as, "It's just a matter of how you feel." "There's no rational way to resolve moral disputes. One can only fight." "Moral claims cannot be true or false." "Morality is just a matter of social convention or prejudice." (Hausman et al. 2016, p. 8).
3. See also Introduction to *The Oxford Handbook of Ethical Theory* (Copp 2005). If we open the latest encyclopedias on business ethics (Werhane and Freeman 2005; Kolb 2007) we also will not see a definite answer on these questions.
4. According to Robert Solomon the majority of textbooks are full of eclectic survey of various approaches and finally "the message to students is too often an unabashed relativism ("if you are a utilitarian, you'll do this, if you're a Kantian, you'll do that")" (Solomon 1992, p. 318)

REFERENCES

Alpay, E. 2011. Student-Inspired Activities for the Teaching and Learning of Engineering Ethics. *Science and Engineering Ethics* 19 (4): 1455–1468.

Børsen, T., A. Antia, and M. Glessmer. 2013. A Case Study of Teaching Social Responsibility to Doctoral Students in the Climate Sciences. *Science and Engineering Ethics* 19 (4): 1491–1504.

Copp, David, ed. 2005. *The Oxford Handbook of Ethical Theory*. New York: Oxford University Press.

Hausman, Daniel, Michael Mcpherson, and Debra Satz. 2016. *Economic Analysis, Moral Philosophy, and Public Policy*. Cambridge University Press.

Holland, Daniel, and Chad Albrecht. 2013. The Worldwide Academic Field of Business Ethics: Scholars' Perceptions of the Most Important Issues. *Journal of Business Ethics* 117 (4): 777–788.

Honderich, Ted, ed. 2005. *The Oxford Companion to Philosophy*. Oxford University Press.

Kolb, R.W., ed. 2007. *Encyclopedia of Business Ethics and Society*. Sage Publications.

Nowell-Smith, P.H. 1952. *Ethics*. London, Penguine Books.

Ozaktas, H. 2011. Teaching Science, Technology, and Society to Engineering Students: A Sixteen Year Journey. *Science and Engineering Ethics* 19 (4): 1439–1450.

Solomon, Robert C. 1992. Corporate Roles, Personal Virtues: An Aristotelean Approach to Business Ethics. *Business Ethics Quarterly* 2 (3): 317–339.

Takala, A.J., and K. Korhonen-Yrjänheikki. 2011. A National Collaboration Process: Finnish Engineering Education for the Benefit of People and Environment. *Science and Engineering Ethics* 19 (4): 1557–1569.

Werhane, Patricia H., and R. Edward Freeman. 2005. *The Blackwell Encyclopedia of Management: Business Ethics*. Malden, MA: Blackwell.

Zandvoort, H., T. Børsen, M. Deneke, and S.J. Bird. 2013. Editors' Overview Perspectives on Teaching Social Responsibility to Students in Science and Engineering. *Science & Engineering Ethics* 19 (4): 1413–1438.

CHAPTER 2

A Scientific Approach to Normative Ethics

Abstract In this chapter we will try to develop our version of a scientific approach to normative ethics. First, we will attempt to define the criteria of science which should be met for a normative framework. Then we will try to develop correct terminology and thereafter to build a series of propositions that should follow from one another in a very strict logical order.

Keywords Normative ethics • Rational choice • Scientific method • Verification • Unanimity • Veil of ignorance

CRITERION OF SCIENTIFIC

This is the key question for further analysis. There are many discussions in the literature about choosing a correct concept of science and a demarcation criterion which helps to distinguish between science and non-science. It would be interesting to analyze normative ethics from the lenses of various perspectives but this should be done in a separate text. Here we will use just one approach—a variant of *positivist concept of science*. Although it was criticized by various authors in the twentieth century it seems that positivism or postpositivism remains a firm and indispensable foundation of contemporary science. What is also important—the main principles of positivist methodology may be well understood by common sense and therefore may be relatively easily articulated to ordinary people who are

© The Author(s) 2018
M. Storchevoy, *A Scientific Approach to Ethics*,
https://Doi.org/10.1007/978-3-319-69113-8_2

the final consumers of our approach. A scientific approach to ethics should be persuasive for ordinary people and that is why it should be based on simple and realistic assumptions.

So, let us develop a simple list of criteria of science which should look very persuasive for students or business people so that no reasonable person can decline any of them. This is my variant of such a list:

- *Accurate definitions.* All terms and concepts of true science should be clearly defined to exclude misunderstanding and wrong judgments. If we say "good," "must," or "justice" everyone should understand these concepts without any ambiguity. Accurate definitions are important to make possible a productive discussion where all participants will understand each other well and will not develop incompatible frameworks.
- *Correct logic.* Theoretical models and explanations should not contain any logical contradiction. If we assume that only individual interests are important we should not suddenly start to speak about interests of the nation. If we assume that everything depends on consequences we cannot start saying that there are good or bad actions as such.
- *Empirical verification.* All theoretical claims or hypotheses should be verified by comparing them to facts and observations. If there is a proposition which is impossible to verify because we do not know what we should measure or observe for this purpose, this proposition is not correctly made or even it is not scientific.
- *Accurate measurement.* When we compare our theoretical predictions with facts we should be sure that we have collected accurate information about facts. For example, if we examine a sample of respondents we should be sure that the sample is representative and has the same characteristics as a general population. Otherwise our verification will be inaccurate.

I have no doubt that there might be other variants of a simple list of criteria but I put the discussion of this problem to the specialists in scientific methodology. For the purpose of our study it is important that every reasonable person (who is the main consumer of a scientific moral philosophy) would rather agree that each of these attributes is a necessary criterion of true science.

All branches of ethics—normative, descriptive, and practical—fit these criteria. The most obvious case is *positive ethics* which already uses methods of other sciences (economics, sociology, psychology) and in which propositions may be checked through proper observations and experiments. *Practical ethics* suggests the methods of regulation which may be verified through experiments (e.g. as in medicine, management or economic policy). What about *normative business ethics*? Here we face the biggest methodological problem. In this chapter, we first examine general normative ethics and demonstrate that it may be rendered in such a way to meet the chosen criteria of science.

BASIC DEFINITIONS

We should start with definitions for two reasons. First, accurate definitions which leave no place for ambiguity are necessary to make possible a productive discussion where all participants understand each other well and do not develop incompatible frameworks (which was the problem with many meta-ethical debates of the twentieth century). Second, a proper choice of definitions is necessary to make the propositions of the theory verifiable.

Let us try to develop such definitions by considering an example. Is it possible to verify a normative proposition "stealing is bad"? It depends on our definition of "stealing" and "bad." There is no problem with an accurate definition of "stealing" which will help to verify if an action is "stealing" or not. We may define it as "expropriating the property of other people without their consent" or "expropriating the results of other people's labor without their consent." This definition may be specified further, but there is no doubt that we can define "stealing" in an accurate way that will help us to classify any action as stealing or non-stealing in an indisputable way.

However, is it possible to define "bad" to make it unambiguous and to create the possibility of verification by observation or logical analysis? What is "bad"? Explaining "bad" in other words we may say that it is "what should not exist." This definition does not seem to be clear because of the word "should." What does it mean? As a consequence, this definition does not allow for verification. We can rephrase the statement "stealing is bad" as "stealing should not exist," but obviously it is unclear how to verify this proposition because of the undefined element "should."

There is only one way to make such a proposition verifiable. We need to add into this definition a *subject*: "bad" is something that should not exist by one's opinion or decision. Here the word "should" gets a clear definition—it means that the person does not want stealing to exist. Therefore, we can build accurate propositions like

- *According to X's opinion, stealing should not exist.*

It is an unambiguous proposition which may be understood as a hypothesis. This hypothesis may be tested logically and empirically. First, we can build some theoretical argumentation on the base of all our knowledge of people's general behavior and particular information about this actor X. Is she rational? What are her interests? Does she understand the consequence of stealing? After a series of logical assumptions we can theoretically derive a conclusion that X does not want stealing to exist. This theoretical model may be *logically checked* and found as correct or wrong.

Second, we can conduct an empirical check of our theoretical hypothesis: we can find the actor X (if it is technically possible) and ask her opinion about stealing. If she asserts that she does not want stealing to exist, this is a valid empirical support of our theoretical claim. Therefore, if normative ethics strictly follows the suggested definitions of "good" and "bad," it can operate with propositions that may be checked for their theoretical correctness and may be empirically verified, which makes normative ethics fit the criteria of science.

ACCURATE CONDITIONS OF INDIVIDUAL CHOICE

There are several additional methodological issues about verification of normative propositions that should be addressed before we can proceed with building a normative ethical theory. If empirical verification of moral propositions is to be conducted by asking the subjects if they really support them, *can the respondents be wrong*? Can a person say "X is good for me" but actually this would be a false statement (mistake) because stealing is actually bad for her. There are two factors that may lead to the alleged mistake: (1) the subject may have various amount of information relevant for this choice, and (2) the subject may be influenced by various emotions. Both factors can definitely influence her judgment. How to account for this problem in our approach? Can we say that the subject should be given full information to make a normative judgment? Can we say that emotions should be excluded from influencing the answer or that they represent relevant moral circumstances? What conditions of choice should be assumed to be necessary for our logical or empirical test? Let us discuss these two factors one by one.

1. *All available information*. Relevant information helps the subject to figure out a fuller number of options, understand better their consequences as well as realize the deeper interests of the actor. So, we may theoretically suggest a general rule—*the more information the subject possesses the more correct judgments she makes about her personal "goods" and "bads."*

Logically, an absolutely correct judgment requires possessing full information about the world. In other words, we may assume that a person will make really true answers about "goods" and "bads" only if she is given full knowledge about everything relevant to the matter of choice. This criterion poses a methodological puzzle because full knowledge of the universe is not feasible, so it is impossible to put actors into the conditions of complete information, and, consequently, it is never possible to get a genuinely true answer on "goods" and "bads"! Does it mean that a scientific approach to science is impossible as well? Although this conclusion is logically true it does not mean that we should adopt a variant of moral error theory assuming that all moral propositions are always wrong because we can never possess all information. Why? First, we may still be interested in revealing moral judgments under the given informational limitations as a moral guide in our practical decisions—this is what business people expect from business ethics and ordinary people expect from general normative ethics. Yes, the genuinely true moral knowledge is unavailable but a best-to-our-knowledge moral truth would have a great value for people. Second, all other "big" sciences like physics or biology operate in the similar circumstances—it is never possible to get the full knowledge of the universe but it does not prevent these sciences from developing themselves and systematic expanding the boundaries of our knowledge. These sciences never possess full information about the world but still they help professional people (engineers or doctors) to base their practical day-to-day decisions on the accumulated knowledge.

Therefore, we can build a variant of scientific normative ethics based on the methodological principle of "all available information"—a moral proposition is correct if the subject supports it after getting all accumulated knowledge about the situation of choice and relevant areas.

Can we prove this methodological principle of "all available information"? We should follow the same verification procedure. Let us build a hypothesis:

- *X wants to possess all available information during making ethical judgments.*

Then let us ask X if she agrees with this proposition. If we are wrong and the subject does not want this, then the "all available information" principle is arbitrary or scientifically unjustified. Logically, it seems that a rational person will prefer to have all relevant information while making decisions about "goods" and "bads." It is obvious that knowledge expands our list of options and understanding of their consequences, so we definitely can improve our decisions knowing more rather than less.

What if a person resists learning all available information before making ethical judgments? Should we accept ethical judgments from this person? It seems not. This is similar to *children's judgments*. A child may think "smoking is good for me" but should we recognize this normative proposition as true? We should not because the child does not possess all relevant information about the consequences of smoking and therefore makes a mistake. Similarly, any person who does not possess all relevant information about the matter of choice *cannot* be a source of verification of normative propositions.

However, there might be also some negative effect to our happiness. Knowledge cannot only change our understanding of the best ways of achieving our goals. It can do much worse—the knowledge may cardinally change *our perception of our interests* because it may turn that our initial view of the world was wrong and we should pursue some other goals or, probably, there are no goals at all that we should pursue. At the same time, it may happen that we will be not able to achieve the same amount of happiness with additional knowledge as we had been achieving without it, or even worse, we cannot be happy at all. For example, a man can be happy thinking that he is immortal and additional knowledge about his inevitable death may seriously change his ability to be happy.

So, the next fundamental hypothesis is:

- *X wants to have all available information about the world, assuming that this may radically change X's current views and destroy some of X's current ideals, values, and expectations?*

Although in reality some people will definitely answer "no" to this question, we can suggest that that the correct answer of a rational person should be positive. There are two arguments justifying the positive answer for this question. First, it seems that *a rational actor is able to manage herself to get the same level of happiness* even if she has some negative knowledge about the future. For example, she can adopt some Stoics techniques and avoid any sort of psychological suffering. Historically, we know that humans were able to get used to any bitter truth and were eventually able to be happy in any circumstances. Second, a *rational actor will realize the opportunity to make better choices* with fuller information. The knowledge of limited span of life will definitely help the person to make wiser allocation of her scarce resources and probably do not postpone some important actions for the future. Logically both explanations (ability to avoid psychological suffering and making better choices) look correct, but we can check this hypothesis by empirical verification. We can conduct an experiment and ask a sample of real persons if they want to have all available information about the world even if they face some bitter truths.

2. *Control of emotions.* An actor's normative judgments may be significantly influenced by her emotions, so we need to account for this factor in our framework. *What emotional conditions should be recognized as leading to true moral judgments?*

The role of emotions in normative judgments was understood quite differently by moral philosophers. Some philosophers claim that emotions reveal the moral truth (we discuss some of these approaches in Chaps. 4, 6 and 7). However, a scientific positive analysis of emotions (see Chap. 3) tells that they represent biological and cultural programs to control behavior of people or make their life easier. Therefore, a rational man should prefer to realize the true nature of emotions and control them from the process of making normative judgments. It does not mean that one should make all decisions contrary to emotions or absolutely neglect emotions, but it means only that *the actor should not be controlled by emotions when making her choice.* The actor may decide to use emotions but it should be a conscious decision (i.e. emotions should be controlled by the actor and not vice versa). Again, this theoretical hypothesis that a rational actor wants to control her emotions looks logically correct, but we need to conduct an empirical test of this hypothesis by asking real people to answer this question.

- *X wants to fully control emotions when making ethical judgments*

If the answer is positive, then we can move further. However, what if a person in our experiment rejects to exclude emotions from the analysis and insists that emotions provide genuine answers for moral questions? Should we take into account normative propositions provided by this respondent?

It seems we should not. We would not take seriously normative judgments of a drunk man or a man under drugs because the reason of that man is distorted by chemicals. Similarly, emotions and feelings (which also have a chemical nature) may distort rational choice. So if a person is driven by emotions and feelings, and cannot break away from their control, her judgments may be treated similar to the judgments of a drunk person. This conclusion may sound a bit scary because it seems like we are building a sort of totalitarian ethics, not giving voice to those who disagree and accusing them of being non-qualified ("inferior") decision makers. However, is this not a normal practice in other areas of our society? A drunk man cannot give witness in court. A scholar in a conference on physics cannot say that she "feels" that some theory is wrong. Opinions of both actors will be excluded as irrelevant by the legal system or scientific community. So why should moral theory give voice to actors whose judgments are distorted by some chemical processes in their bodies and who refuse to recognize this fact? Another analogy would be our attitude to children's judgments. A child may desperately and ultimately insist that "smoking is good for me" but should we recognize this normative proposition as true? It seems that we should not because the child does not possess all relevant information about the consequences of smoking and has not learned to control her emotions yet, so she may easily make a wrong choice. Similarly, a person of any age who does not possess all relevant information about the matter of choice, or who cannot control her emotions, cannot be a source of verification of normative propositions.

Therefore, we suggest that derivation of moral propositions about "goods" and "bads" requires controlling two factors—information and emotions. The true moral propositions must be made under full available information and under full control of emotions.

UNIVERSAL MORAL NORMS

All previous discussion was focused only on the possibility of scientific verification of individual moral propositions about "goods" and "bads." In other words we dealt only with subjective moral truths of a particular person. The next question should be: *Is it possible to derive universal moral propositions?* We can define universal moral propositions as moral judgments which are evaluated as true by everyone. Such universal moral proposition may be an evaluation of some object or action (e.g. "economic growth should be high"), or a universal norm of behavior (e.g. "no one should abuse market power"). In both cases, by definition this moral proposition may be called a universal moral truth if and only if everyone supports it. Are these propositions possible?

EXISTENCE OF UNIVERSAL MORAL NORMS

It can be argued logically that universal moral propositions are possible. The mere existence of such propositions may be proved by taking some obvious examples of such propositions that should be supported by everyone, e. g. "global nuclear war should not happen," "this world should exist." No rational subject will deny that these moral propositions are true from her subjective point of view. Again, we assume two conditions from the previous analysis—all available information and control of emotions (e.g. a follower of a doomsday cult or an unhappy lover may wish death to all people but we should not take these judgments into account).

However, there are much less obvious cases that may lead to disputes between people where it will be more difficult to reveal if a moral proposition is universal or not. Therefore, we should define *correct criteria for testing a particular moral proposition for being a universal one.* There should be several conditions. First, we should use two conditions from the previous analysis—*all available information* and *control of emotions*. So, we can suggest that a rational person will be interested in the existence of universal moral norms which tell people what is right and what is wrong. We can verify this claim in a more obvious form by testing this hypothesis:

- *X wills that there should be universal moral norms which all people should obey*

It seems that a rational answer should be positive, because it is logical to assume that these moral norms will protect the values and interests of the person. For example, norms prohibiting violence protect everyone from such actions. It seems that the mere existence of laws in any society supports this hypothesis, because laws are universal compulsory moral norms.

At this moment, we do not say what particular norms should exist, but ask about the mere existence of *some* moral norms. However, when we try to define *what* moral norms should exist, we may face some disagreement between people. To resolve these problems we should carefully specify a *morally correct procedure* for choosing moral norms which will be agreed upon by all people. This procedure has several characteristics which we will discuss one by one.

Procedure of Choice: Who?

First of all, we need to specify WHO should define the universal moral norms that people want. Should moral norms be chosen by people or taken from some other source (divine revelation, etc.).

- *X wants that moral norms should be determined by people.*

What about divine revelation or religious sources? Why not take moral norms from the Bible or Quran? It seems that the rational person will agree to use these sources as a reference because they accumulate some ancient wisdom but will not use them as an ultimate source of truth. First, a rational scientific analysis of consequences of any action works much better that a religious source, which is oversimplified and sometimes may be wrong. Second, how can we achieve an agreement on universal moral norms in the society with many religions? Finally, if we want to build a scientific moral theory it seems hardly possible to borrow any moral truth from unscientific sources such as religion.

Procedure of Choice: All People?

The next question is: should all people participate in the process of norms choice or some people should be excluded? By definition, it is very important for universal moral norms to be supported by all people. However, what if some people make a wrong choice?

As discussed earlier, wrong answers may be given by people who do not have all available information or who are controlled by emotions. We suggested that a rational person will prefer to get all available information and be able to control emotions, but in reality some may refuse to do this. There are two categories of people who fit this category: people with psychological disorders (e.g. those who cannot make rational choices), or people not willing to educate themselves. However, this is a difficult methodological question because there are many types of mental disorders—the American Psychiatric Association approved a list of over 450 types. What criterion should be used to reveal those who should be excluded?

Here moral philosophy may try to borrow the experience of law where any actor is admitted to participate in the legal process (e.g. trial) only if one has *competence*—the mental capacity to participate in legal proceedings or transactions and to be responsible for his or her decisions or acts. If a person does not have competence, she will be excluded from legal process or even subjected to involuntary commitment (put into a hospital for the mentally ill). There are various competences: competence to stand trial, competence to enter into a contract, etc. Scientific ethics may examine this approach and develop its own criteria for *competency to choose moral norms*.

Procedure of Choice: Unanimity?

The next question is: should the norms be approved unanimously or we can use some other rule, e.g. simple or qualified majority? It seems that we should use the unanimous rule because by definition universal rules should be accepted by everyone, otherwise they cease to be universal. This is the power of scientific approach to ethics because everyone should be shown that he or she actually supports the universal moral norm. At the same time representatives of any minority have the right to block any moral norm which violates their interests. To verify this question we should ask the person:

- *X wants that universal moral norms should be adopted unanimously.*

Procedure of Choice: Veil of Ignorance?

Now there is the problem of *different needs and capabilities*. Even if various people have all available information and full control of emotions they still may give different answers about universal norms because they have different personal preferences, talents, and wealth. For example, rich people will prefer zero or low taxes, but poor people will require high ones on the rich. The monopolist will choose no regulation of pricing under monopoly but her consumers will vote for a strict regulative policy. The employer will vote for a low minimum wage, but the employees will desire a higher one. There will be many disagreements and even conflicts about universal norms.

The solution against this situation is to design a moral procedure of achieving agreement about universal moral norms (e.g. level of taxes) which will be supported by everyone and will be a universal moral norm itself.

A good candidate for this universal moral norm is *veil of ignorance* (Harsanyi 1953; Rawls 1971)—we need to put all people in the original position (under a veil of ignorance) where no one knows her needs and capabilities in the real world. In this situation people will try to defend themselves from suffering in the most vulnerable positions and will try to improve these positions as much as possible (e.g. will set up taxes at the level that maximizes support of the needy but does not hamper economic growth). Rawls called this condition of choice "fair" because no one uses her advantages (this is a definition of fairness in this context). It is interesting to notice that our first condition of moral choice requires providing all available information to the person, but the condition of fairness requires us to take some information from people to guarantee that their choice will be moral. However, the veil of ignorance concept cannot be that this proposition should be scientifically proved as all other propositions in our theory. Can we prove logically and empirically that every subject will support veil of ignorance as the best procedure of achieving agreement about universal norms? This is one of the most difficult tasks of a scientific ethics. It is easy to persuade the poor or weak person to support veil of ignorance, but how to persuade wealthy and healthy people? Essentially, it means to persuade people to sacrifice part of their welfare for the sake of others.

What arguments may we use? We cannot use emotional appeal to push their feelings about fairness, human dignity or compassion, because our second condition requires them to control their emotions, so this instrument is unavailable. The only argument compatible with rational choice is the uncertainty of the future. This argument may be represented in two parts. First, even the wealthiest and mightiest person cannot be absolutely sure that the social or natural environment will not change in the future in an unfavorable way and she will find herself in a very vulnerable position. So, the rational choice would be to insure oneself from these risks and to protect the vulnerable positions in the society in advance. Second, if a subject wants to protect not only herself but her children, grandchildren, and other descendants, then the chances for accepting the third condition increase. The longer is perspective the higher is uncertainty, and the higher are the chances that one's descendant will find themselves in the vulnerable positions of the society. Therefore, a rational choice would be to establish universal moral norms that protect these positions. In other words, the veil of ignorance is not just a thought experiment, *it is really created by uncertainty of the future*, and we need just to explain this to people. Theoretically, this logic looks correct, but to support it empirically we should run an experiment with real people who will need to evaluate this norm according to our conditions.

- *X wants to use Veil of Ignorance as a procedure of universal moral norms choice*

EMPIRICAL VERIFICATION

All propositions of scientific normative ethics should be empirically verified by asking real people to agree or disagree with each of them. This is not an easy process because people should get enough knowledge to qualify as respondents in this empirical test. Another problem is that various people will react differently to these propositions. Even if these propositions are actually true and all people will eventually agree with them, every person may initially disagree at some specific moment and will require corresponding clarifications and arguments that will persuade every person that a proposition is true. Therefore, empirical verification requires two things: (1) educational texts that may be used by respondents to get necessary knowledge if needed, (2) a scenario of questions that should be asked to respondents if they disagree with any proposition. We may call this scenario *Socratic flowchart* because it should be built like a Socratic dialogue—a sequence of questions which anticipates all potential directions of discussion and which eventually leads to the final proposition. It should be organized as a flowchart which anticipates all potential rejections or misunderstandings which could be met and resolved with Socratic questions and eventually gets the respondent back to the backbone logic of moral theory.

Although this framework is essentially based on the unanimity principle and requires consent of all people in society, we do not really need to ask *all society members* if they agree. The latter would be impossible from one hand and unnecessary from the other hand. Many scientific empirical researches are based on examination of representative samples. We may build a representative sample for our task and check if everyone agrees with our propositions.

If any member of society does not trust our results proven on the representative sample, she is invited to go through the same Socratic flowchart. If the person does not agree with one of our propositions she should prove the opposite. If she does not have enough time for exploring all necessary educational text and to think about all questions which will be raised by a Socratic flowchart, she may refuse to start this process or stop at any moment but in this case she should accept the condition: "I prefer to stop this process and trust the result of scientific analysis." If she does not want to go through a Socratic flowchart and does not want to prove that some proposition is wrong, but still disagree with our final conclusion, she will look silly. The same situation takes place with any other science—e.g. you should trust medicine and accept its conclusions or should study all necessary medical literature to understand them. But you cannot just say that medicine is wrong.

Although the idea of scientific normative ethics may look too radical, it is actually not a revolution but a last small step to assemble together the tools and concepts of various traditions (rational choice, contractualism, Socratic methods, etc.). Moreover, this method eventually leads to similar answers as many other traditions do. The only difference is that now it is assembled in accordance with scientific method.

REFERENCES

Harsanyi, John. 1953. Cardinal Utility in Welfare Economics and in the Theory of Risk-Taking. *Journal of Political Economy* 61 (5): 434–435.

Rawls, John. 1971. *A Theory of Justice*. Harvard University Press.

CHAPTER 3

Evolutionary Model of Man

Abstract In this chapter we will discuss the evolutionary model of man which represents a scientific explanation of man, his desires, feelings, and rationality. These factors are important to develop positive ethics (to explain why people have senses of justice and how they make moral choices), normative ethics (to understand better values and goals which people may have) and practical ethics (to shape better educational or regulatory policies).

Keywords Evolution • Rationality • Instincts • Emotions • Rational choice • Ethics

The scientific approach to ethics needs a correct understanding of people's behavior and the mechanism of their choices. What is rational behavior and what is not? Why do our emotions influence our decisions and how should we deal with that? Should we recognize feelings as a source of true morality?

For quite a long time various social sciences have studied man in their own manner. *Economists* modeled man as a rational actor who tries to maximize his utility function and takes conscious rational decisions about everything in an attempt to achieve this goal. All emotional and cultural influences were understood as external non-rational factors which mostly distort the maximizing choice. *Sociologists* saw man as a social actor who wants to be legitimate and tries to comply with social norms. They emphasized that

© The Author(s) 2018
M. Storchevoy, *A Scientific Approach to Ethics*,
https://doi.org/10.1007/978-3-319-69113-8_3

people are not autonomous in their choice but shaped by social reality. *Psychology* and *biology* were focused on functioning of brain and body without much attention to social factors. *Moral philosophers* studied human consciousness in their own way—mostly introspectively, basing on their own psychological experience and attitudes.

However, by the end of the twentieth century social sciences accumulated much knowledge to abandon this isolation and build a new model of man which would reconcile different views and concepts. In this chapter I will suggest an *evolutionary model of man* which is built as a modification of the traditional economic model of man. The economic model of man is a good start because it focuses on people's choice and evaluation of this choice. What we need to do is to modify its target function—the real purpose of man should not be maximization of utility function but survival. And we need to include emotions and culture as central factors of choice which help to achieve this ultimate purpose.

THREE LEVELS OF CHOICE

The whole process of choice in the new model may be depicted as a hierarchy of three levels—biological, cultural, and rational (see Fig. 3.1). Every decision is made at all three levels but the comparative influence of each level may vary in different situations.

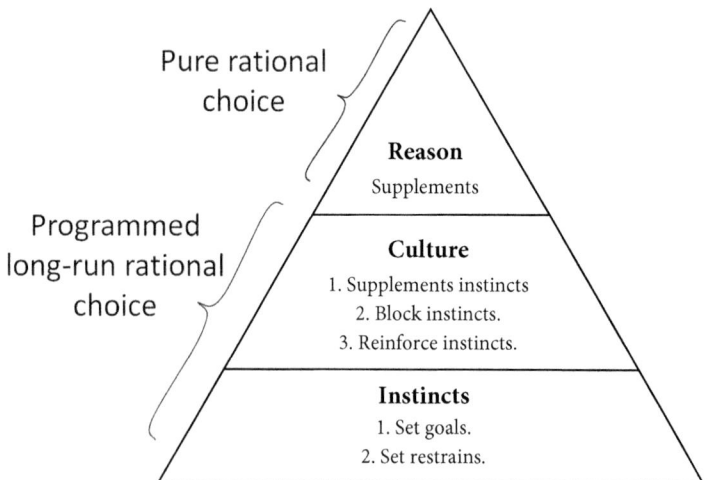

Fig. 3.1   Three levels of choice

The bottom level is biological *instincts* which are genetically inherited by the man from his ancestors and serve two main functions: (1) set purposes (food, water, safety, warmth, etc.) and (2) set restrictions (e.g. fear of death). They are like *hardware* in computer—a man is born with hardwired "chips" and cannot change them during one's life. All emotions of man (fear, anger, sympathy, etc.) are programmed at this level.

The middle level of choice is *culture*—norms and values which every human gets during childhood and socialization. The main function of culture is to adapt instincts to certain social environments. They may do three things: (1) supplement instincts when the latter are insufficient (e.g. fear of electricity is absent in instincts and developed by culture), (2) reinforce instincts (instinctive desire to avoid dirt may be reinforced by cultural norms of hygiene), and (3) block instincts (e.g. natural aggression is blocked in contemporary culture). Cultural norms may be interpreted as *software* which is downloaded into the hardware to complement, reinforce, or block its functions and achieve better results. They *can evolve* during human life and may be consciously adjusted by reason.

The top level of the hierarchy is *reason* or *intellect* which makes conscious logical decisions about the best way to achieving a goal. At first it seems natural to compare reason with the operator of the computer, but this is not so. Reason is only a processor or CPU which performs the logical operations trying to achieve purposes set by instincts and culture under limitations defined by instincts and culture. The only difference with a computer processor is that human reason can recognize itself and to write these words which you are reading.

Let us now explain how this model works and provides rational choice. Rational choice is the decision which leads to achievement the purpose.

1. *Survival instead of maximization.* The target function of this model is not maximization of utility or happiness but survival. So, the choice is rational if it leads the man to survival.

2. *Two mechanisms of choice.* There are two mechanisms of making "choice": (1) *conscious choice* (decisions made by reason to achieve given purposes) and (2) *natural selection choice* (a blind "choice" made by evolutionary mechanism where instincts and culture norms are "chosen" through the process of competition and survival of the fittest).

3. *Instincts compensate for the limitations of reason.* Reason can make wrong decisions because of limited computing ability and information (bounded rationality). Instincts should block these decisions and to drive man to a right choice.
4. *0 compensates for the limited instincts.* Instincts were formed at the primitive stage of the development of society. They can be ineffective in a modern economy with a developed legal system and new sophisticated situations of choice (like in financial markets).

This model can explain not only behavior of real people but their constitution, or answer the question why Homo Sapiens have all these feelings, emotions, cultural norms, and other elements of choice.

To explain any instinct or cultural norm we should two questions. First, *is this instinct/norm rational?* A rational norm should help to survive in the long run. For example, the instinct of hunger sends signal that there is shortage of energy in the body which should be topped up. Second, *why should this instinct/norm be programmed?* If reason understands that food is necessary for energy, instinct is not necessary anymore? However your reason is bounded and can make mistakes, so it should be blocked and driven to the correct action. For example, in the situation of shortage of energy you may decide that you can eat later and continue to do more interesting things instead of searching food. This will have fatal consequences because at some moment you may have not enough energy to find the food and die. To prevent this mistake that may be made by your reason, your instincts block your reason and make it search food. This is an explanation of why the instinct of hunger is rational.

We can try to explain in the same way all other instincts and cultural norms including those which have primary importance for ethics. For example, *sense of honesty*—many people have negative feelings when they are going to tell lies. Is it rational? In a vast majority situations it is rational because you achieve two good purposes: (1) you build good personal reputation and people will be happy to deal with you in the future and (2) you promote honest behavior in the community and will benefit from honesty of other people in the future. Why should this strategy be programmed? Because human intellect is shortsighted and may underestimate the long-term consequences. For example, you can lie to a partner and get big benefits hoping that the partner will never know about this. However, you cannot foresee all future events and when the lie becomes known your future destiny is under threat. So, reason can make a mistake and should be blocked by negative emotions from telling lies. It is interesting that anti-lies programming occurs at the cultural level of the hierarchy because there is no biological instinct of honesty. People from underdeveloped economies very often demonstrate low level of honesty in contractual relations and are prone to cheating in many forms. Developed societies have a much better established cultural norm of honesty but they may demonstrate a significant variation in the level of adoption of this norm depending on their professional culture. For example, the empirical studies of students' integrity shows that the business and economics disciplines increase readiness of students to cheat. In 1964 W. Bowers, who surveyed about 5000 students from 99 campuses, found out that cheating was resorted to by 66% of students in business schools which was 16% higher than the average rate of about 50% (Bowers 1964). In 1997 Donald McCabe examined 16 universities and found out that cheating was confessed by 84% of business schools students and 72% of engineering students with an average rate of 66% for the whole population. In 2006 the survey of 5000 students from 32 universities showed that the maximum propensity for cheating was still demonstrated by business students (about 26% confessed in cheating on an exam, 54% in plagiarism during homework). The highest integrity was demonstrated by the students of natural sciences (about 26% confessed in cheating). However, these observations may be interpreted in two different ways. First, students' behavior changes with education and any normal student after joining a business school becomes less honest. This explanation is supported by Ghoshal (2005) and the research of Aspen Institute shows that during the two-year MBA program value attitudes of student's shifts from caring about customers and product quality to caring about the shareholders' value as the ultimate criteria of company's performance (Aspen Institute 2003). Second, this observation may be partly explained by self-selection which takes place at the stage of entering the business school.

OPTIMIZATION FEELINGS

There are several instincts that may be loosely named as optimization capabilities because they regulate decisions about quantities or scales. For example, the instinct of *risk aversion* regulates behavior in risky situations making the person avoid any options which may have losses dangerous for welfare and survival. Even when probabilities of all outcomes are known and the expected reward is positive people may refuse to play into a game because their psychological evaluation of losses is higher than of rewards (in behavioral economics this is known as prospect theory, developed by Kahneman and Tversky in 1979). This instinctive behavior may be explained as a result of survival of those people who tried to completely exclude the possibility of negative outcomes. An interesting experiment was run by researchers in the new field of neuroeconomics . Shiv et al. (2005) explored behavior of people with damaged brains—the area responsible for fear did not function, although their intellectual capabilities and IQ level were quite normal. They were compared with the second group of people with normal brains. Participants played the game: everyone got 20 dollars and the option to participate in 20 rounds of investment decisions. At each round the participant had two options: invest $1 or save $1. Then a coin was flipped and the participant earned $2.5 for the head and nothing for the tail. The rational choice would be investing every round because the expected value of this lottery is $1.25 which is more than $1. The surprising thing—the people with damaged brain made more advantageous investments because normal people often declined to invest for some time after consequent loss in two or three rounds. It follows that instinct of risk aversion leads to wrong decisions in financial markets rather than a pure rational choice! However, the rationality of an instinct should be tested in the long run but not in one specific experiment. In the long run the normal people with instinct of risk aversion may perform "fearless" competitors. This guess is well supported by the evidence of the same experiment—the majority of the people with damaged brain in these experiments had *experienced personal bankruptcy* at least once in their life. Therefore, the instinct of risk aversion is a good safety device.

Another optimization feeling is *greed*—a desire to appropriate much more resources than is necessary for satisfying current needs. Usually greed is considered as a negative trait of human character but it may be argued that greed is also an evolutionary effective trait. Man cannot predict the future and that is why it is always a good idea to accumulate some resources as a safety stock. This is rational and it is should be programed because a "rational" mind can be misguided by a stable and favorable present and fail to predict the future deficit. The instinct of greed makes man accumulate a safety stock. This instinct has dual consequences for the market economy. On the one hand, it coincides with the purpose of profit maximization which leads to efficient allocation of resources (Invisible hand by Adam Smith or "Greed is good" by Gordon Gekko). On the other hand, it leads to luxurious and conspicuous consumption which may be seen as a waste of resources and it often leads to violation of moral norms because very high financial reward may distort the perception of reality of a normal manager and push him to violation of legal and moral norms.

POSITIVE FEELINGS

There are several instinctive types of positive behavior toward other people that also may be explained on the basis of evolutionary model. A person may have very deep feelings toward someone of (usually) opposite sex which may be called *love*. A person can have warm feelings toward other people of the same or the opposite sex which is called *friendship*. A person can have positive feelings to complete strangers and to their country. In all these cases people are ready to sacrifice part of their welfare in the interest of other people. Can we explain this behavior on the basis of the evolutionary model?

There are two types of *love*: (1) strong romantic and sexual attraction which develops rather fast (few days or weeks) and vanishes rather fast, (2) a deep psychological feeling of spiritual intimacy which develops in years and stays for a very long time. Both types fit the evolutionary model pretty well. *Romantic love* is an instinct that makes a person put off other business to create a family even if the person would prefer to delay it for a later time or does not want it at all. Moreover, the instinct of romantic love helps the person find an appropriate partner. For example, empirical research shows that scent preferences correspond with genetic compatibility (Penn 2002). It may be argued that other type of instinctive preferences (type of face, hair, etc.) also may reflect not-observed genetic compatibility. Another explanation is that romantic love generates energy to win the heart of your partner and overcome a variety of other circumstances to create a family. When the family is created, romantic love is no longer necessary and it should normally be replaced by *family love* which is crucial in the long run. Living your whole life together with some other person requires you to have some positive feelings toward this person which will help you to overcome everyday problems that may arise in the relationships (including the quite challenging task of raising kids). Moreover, the best partner for raising kids is their second parent who is interested in the success of this project much more than any other potential partners. Both romantic love and family love are rational but a person cannot evoke them deliberately. One needs instinctive capabilities to have these experiences and become an effective partner in relationships that is why they are programmed.

What about friendship? Usually we experience a lot of positive emotions toward our *friends* who share with us their feelings, thoughts, ideas, secrets, leisure, etc. Why do we need friends if we do not make kids with them? Actually the answer is exactly the opposite—the friend may take care of your children in hard times. The friend may provide support which will not be available from strangers. In the case of unexpected financial troubles friends are the most efficient credit institution which will not ask any questions about pledge and will charge zero rate of interest. As primatologists have found (Silk et al. 2003) sociality of adult females of wild baboons is positively associated with infant survival. In other words those females who form strong bonds with kin and other group members increase the survival chances of their brood.

Sometime people provide help not to their family members or friends but to *strangers*. There are various theories of reciprocal altruism that try to explain this behavior. In the 1960s the evolutionary biologist W. Hamilton suggested the theory of kin selection where readiness to help depends on the extent of the relatedness of the species. In 1971 Robert Trivers suggested readiness to help depends on the probability to get similar help in the future, so this norm may evolve only in small societies (historically the human race developed in such small communities) (Trivers 1971). In 1998 Sober and Wilson suggested the theory of group selection which suggests that readiness to help people from the same community seriously increases chances of survival in aggressive competition with other communities (Sober and Wilson 1998). This altruism is created by culture and not instincts. An interesting example of this is the history of two plagues that hurt the Roman Empire in 165–180 and 251–266 AD. Both Christian and pagan communities were affected by these plagues but the former survived much better than the latter. Why? Large numbers of pagans, including rulers, priests, and physicians, fled to get away from the plague. Unlike the pagans, most Christians followed new moral norms of mutual help and caring about the neighbors. They stayed and helped each other as well as ill pagans. According to epidemiologists, basic health care, such as providing pure water and adequate warmth, can result in as much as a 30% higher survival rate. Pagans observed this "miracle," and, as a result, conversion rates from paganism to Christianity soared.

NEGATIVE FEELINGS

When a person faces a difficult task—a physically hard action or a fight with a serious enemy—she often has feelings of *anger* toward this task. Why? This instinct helps the person to spend a larger amount of energy in a rather short period of time to overcome all hardships and to solve the task. This "turbo mode" is a rational instinct but why should it be programmed? One possible answer is that reason cannot activate these hidden capacities directly. This mode is activated only by the emotional trigger. However, this instinct seems to be present in many animals. Under attack from a very dangerous enemy, animals start to protect themselves with incredible amount of energy. Especially if the enemy threatens their children. Humans inherited anger and may benefit from its existence because they still need to overcome some physically or intellectually difficult problem, but may also suffer from this emotion (e.g. anger management courses).

When a person receives material or psychological damage from another person he feels automatic negative emotions which force him to wish a similar damage toward the "offender." This is an *instinct of revengefulness.* Is it rational? It is because anticipation of inevitable revenge stops offenders. The revenge itself is a destructive action which hardly could be called a good thing, but its main benefit is not revenge itself but anticipation of inevitable revenge which prevents offense. If revengefulness is rational why should it be programmed? Again reason may fail to make this choice. First, revengefulness was programmed at the early stage of evolution when the reason of human beings was underdeveloped and the benefits of revenge may not have been realized. Second, even intellect of modern man may underestimate the importance of revenge or take a shortsighted decision of avoiding short-term costs of revenge which may be high.

We may note that revengefulness is regulated both by instincts and culture. There is a tradition of *blood revenge* in some oriental societies which serves a function limiting the scope of revenge which otherwise may lead to a spiral of increasing mutual revengeful actions and a devastating conflict. In developed countries the function of revenge was completely transferred to *tort law* because this replace the costly emotional mechanism of personal revenge with a cheaper and more effective system (even the weakest member of society is protected). Now cultural norms in developed countries block the biological instinct of revengefulness.

An offended person may have bitter feelings and prefer not to revenge but to refrain from any further interaction with the offender. It may be called an instinct of *resentfulness* and its rationale is also clear—continuing relations with a bad partner is not a good idea. Why should this instinct be programmed? Again, probably this reaction was programmed at the early stages of human development when the reason was weak for such extrapolations. An alternative explanation is that resentfulness may be relevant in the relationship between lovers or friends where people have strong inclination to each other. Therefore, to send a clear signal to the partner about inappropriate behavior one needs to be seriously upset and ready to withdraw from relationships for some time.

Cardinal Feelings

Some instincts have a fundamental role in the life of the human being that is why we can call them *cardinal feelings* (by analogy with cardinal virtues). These are feelings of happiness, sense of duty and religious feeling.

Happiness, or more precisely *the ability to experience happiness or unhappiness*, is a fundamental biological or cultural program which should reward the person for the efforts spent to achieve a purpose. It should be noted that there are already some direct rewards for vital actions. For example, if a person is hungry and finds the food, he is rewarded with the pleasure of eating. The same goes for thirst and all other material needs. Why should evolution create additional reward if satisfaction of any particular need is rewarded by direct pleasures? There is only one plausible answer: the sense of happiness is a special reward for achievements in *non-material cognitive space* which is constructed by the society. This is a space of such ideal concepts as goods and bads, friends and enemies, success and failure. Reward for achievements in this field cannot be a direct physiological consequence of some physical actions as with satisfying needs in food or water. That is why people created the concept of "success." Achieving this state leads to the feeling of "happiness." Sure, this feeling is also based on physiologic processes but the *trigger* of this sense is fully cognitive and socially constructed. This capability to experience happiness might play a fundamental role in human evolution because it provided a mechanism for social development through competition in a non-material space.

Sense of duty is activated when a person is thinking about breaking a moral norm and transfers in the *sense of guilt* if the person decides to do this. Is it rational? It is because following moral norms is generally rational.

Why should it be programmed? Again, as in the case with honesty, the intellect may be an insufficient judge in such situations and may push a person to break a norm. If a person has no experience of relationships in a certain environment (e.g. the person is young), he may not realize all consequences of breaking a norm. In this case negative emotions create extra costs and make him follow norms.

Religious feeling allows people to experience the presence of God which is very important for enforcement of a religious moral code. The fear of punishment for sins and the internal reward for living a good life are incredibly effective mechanisms of promoting moral behavior. A religious society with a good moral code can easily outperform other societies without such codes and win the competitive struggle for resources. Therefore, those people who have strong religious feeling are effective in evolutionary competition.

It is important to note that all three cardinal instincts (instinct of happiness, sense of duty, and religious feelings) exist as biological capabilities but should be developed and maintained through cultural norms (secular ideologies or religion) without which they can hardly function. Instincts and culture often act together to control reason and avoid mistakes.

IMPLICATIONS FOR NORMATIVE ETHICS

The evolutionary model of man provides a scientific explanation of people's behavior which is quite important for developing a more grounded normative ethics. There are several implications.

First, all emotions and intuitions of man do not reveal any fundamental moral truth, they are just useful programs for controlling human behavior. Emotional or intuitive choice (e.g. altruism) may coincide with the moral choice made by scientific ethics which is built exclusively on reason, but it cannot be a source of moral justification as such.

Second, a moral philosopher while developing a normative theory should completely abstain from any emotions and feelings (a condition violated by many). If a moral theory is based on emotions or intuitions it does not meet the criteria of scientific method, even if its conclusions coincide with the conclusions of the latter.

Third, according to the evolutionary model of man the only purpose of life is to survive and leave offspring. Does this conclusion influence decisions of the rational actor in building normative propositions (Chap. 2), i.e. definitions of good, derivation of universal moral norms, etc.? It does not because regardless of the purpose of human life or the role of emotions the answers to all questions will be the same.

Fourth, should a rational person agree to perform the program which is given to her by nature or may she rebel and declare her own purposes? As far as the rational person in our theory is already a grown, educated adult, she has three options: (1) continue to fulfill biological-cultural programs, (2) escape and maximize personal utility, and (3) stop living. What will a rational person choose regardless of moral considerations? It depends on the relative well-being of this person. If she enjoys her life she will choose between 1 and 2, if she is suffering she may chose 3. What *ought* a rational person to choose? A rational person should ask what moral norm she would like to have for this situation under veil of ignorance. Here we expand our theoretical experiment from the previous chapter and add a temporal dimension and the child-parent relationship. There are three types of actors who are directly involved in this dilemma: (1) all ancestors of this person, (2) the person, and (3) all descendants of this person who may be born. The person should choose the norm about performing or rejecting the biological program not knowing which position she will take: (1) ancestors who already performed this program, (2) the person who is going to make this choice, or (3) descendants who may be born as the result of this decision. The dead ancestors would probably answer that they do not care because all their decisions have already been made and nothing will change in their past lives. The living ancestors will prefer if we continued the biological-cultural program because it would make their lives easier and happier. The living descendants (if the person already has kids) will agree with living ancestors. The unborn descendants probably will want to be born if they also may live happy lives. Can we empirically verify these hypotheses? We cannot ask dead ancestors, so our hypothesis about their choice may be tested only by asking living people if they agree with our logic. Living ancestors and descendants can be asked with certainty, and unborn descendants may be asked ex post if we decide to give them life. So, this proposition is also empirically verifiable. However, this normative analysis is not complete because we should consider as our stakeholders all *other people* who are living and may be living in the future. Some of them may need our help because of some natural or economic problems. They may be defined as the most vulnerable people in this situation. So under veil of ignorance a rational person should vote for moral norms which improves the welfare of these people. Therefore, any person should continue to live, fulfill her biological-cultural programs, and help those who need her help. This is not a complete analysis of this problem but only the idea how it may be approached on the basis of scientific ethics.

Fifth, the evolutionary model of man suggests new theoretical insights for virtue ethics. A scientific study of instincts and cultural norms in the evolutionary model of man may help to elaborate the concept of virtue in virtue ethics. Probably, we can refine the list of virtues, understanding better their nature, and figure out a better practical approach for developing and promoting virtuous behavior. The evolutionary model of man may help to rethink the concept of *golden mean* as suggested by Aristotle, who thought that every character trait becomes a virtue only when it is exercised in between two extremes. In the evolutionary model many instincts and cultural norms also may be followed with various degrees of intensity and the *best evolutionary result* is achieved when the person finds an *optimum amount of action* for any instinct and norm. For example, if the person tries to realize a maximum amount of altruism toward strangers, he will have to give up all personal resources to strangers and fail to achieve his own purposes. If the person starts using too much anger in every task he may lose too much energy on unimportant tasks. Aristotle did not leave an explicit criterion for finding the golden mean and defined it simply as avoiding extremes. Probably, the evolutionary model can shed additional light on this criterion. These are good questions for a further discussion.

REFERENCES

Aspen Institute. 2003. *Where Will They Lead: MBA Student Attitudes about Business and Society.* https://www.aspeninstitute.org

Bowers, William J. 1964. *Student Dishonesty and Its Control in College.* New York: Bureau of Applied Social Research, Columbia University.

Ghoshal, Sumantra. 2005. Bad Management Theories are Destroying Good Management Practice. *Academy of Management Learning and Education* 4 (1): 75–91.

Kahneman, Daniel, and Amos Tversky. 1979. Prospect Theory: An Analysis of Decision Under Risk. *Econometrica: Journal of the Econometric Society* 47 (2): 263–291.

Penn, Dustin J. 2002. The Scent of Genetic Compatibility: Sexual Selection and the Major Histocompatibility Complex. *Ethology* 108 (1): 1–21.

Shiv, B., G. Loewenstein, A. Bechara, H. Damasio, and A.R. Damasio. 2005. Investment Behavior and the Negative Side of Emotion. *Psychological Science* 16 (6): 435–439.

Silk, J.B., S.C. Alberts, and J. Altmann. 2003. Social Bonds of Female Baboons Enhance Infant Survival. *Science* 302 (5648): 1231–1234.

Sober, Elliott, and David Sloan Wilson. 1998. *Unto Others: The Evolution and Psychology of Unselfish Behavior.* Cambridge, MA: Harvard University Press.

Trivers, R.L. 1971. The Evolution of Reciprocal Altruism. *Quarterly Review of Biology* 46: 35–57.

CHAPTER 4

Normative Ethics Before the Twentieth Century

Abstract In this chapter we will explore the most interesting period in the development of ethics—the appearance of the idea of science and the following construction of a new type of knowledge based only on rational argumentation. We will explore how the creators of the new human knowledge understood the methodological status of ethics and will see that surprisingly many of them believed in the possibility of building a scientific variant of ethics. Other philosophers took opposite positions and claimed that scientific ethics was impossible. Later this skepticism had a strong influence on further development of moral philosophy and other social sciences.

Keywords Utilitarianism • Social contract • Natural law • Sense of beauty • Ethics • Scientific method • Scholastic • Skepticism

Ancient Ethics

Although there had been no idea of science in ancient times, many ancient philosophers were in tune with assumptions of scientific ethics because they preferred the life of reason and rational thought. There were proto-scientific explanations of the natural world (e.g. atomism) and of ethical issues. Let us outline them briefly.

Socrates made two important contributions. First, he emphasized reason and logic as essential tools to discover truths in life. Second, he developed the idea of persuasion in disputes (Socratic dialogue) which may be used as a principal tool in verification in scientific ethics (see Chap. 2). Third, Socrates assumed that nobody wants to commit evil and if one does evil it happens only because of ignorance. This is exactly the idea of having all available information when making a choice in the scientific approach to ethics.

Plato believed that there is objective knowledge about good (Form of the Good) that theoretically can be known although it is very difficult and no one could know it yet. Although it may seem as a prototype of a scientific approach to ethics that assumes objective moral knowledge, it was actually a non-scientific approach because we lack an accurate definition of good (what we are looking for) and it is unclear how propositions about it may be falsified.

Aristotle is known as a great contributor to virtue ethics and implicitly used a rational method of justification of virtues but it was mostly a contribution to positive ethics. He was rather skeptical about the possibility of a strict approach to ethics. In the beginning of *The Nicomachean Ethics* he made a reservation about methodological difference of ethics where all knowledge is established by convention between people and not by nature. However, there is much variety and fluctuation of opinion and there is no way to find universal truth.

> ... for it is the mark of an educated man to look for precision in each class of things just so far as the nature of the subject admits; it is evidently equally foolish to accept probable reasoning from a mathematician and to demand from a rhetorician scientific proofs. (*The Nicomachean Ethics*, Book I, chapter 3)

Epicurus came very close to scientific ethics. He had a materialistic approach to philosophy based on logic and observation. His atomic theory of the universe and materialistic theory of soul were explained exclusively with logical arguments. Elizabeth Asmis in her book *Epicurus' Scientific Method* (1984) tried to demonstrate that Epicurus did have a coherent method of scientific inference far beyond anything that classicists and scientists have hitherto acknowledged. In moral philosophy this approach led to predictable outcome—a subjective theory of rational choice. As far as people are on their own in this world and there is no life after death, they have to make the only reasonable choice—to get the pleasure from what they can.

This rational approach to ethics of life was partly inherited by *Stoics* who developed many arguments and techniques for avoiding non-rational suffering during human life. However, general methodology of Stoics was far from scientific, because they believed in "world's reason" which is diluted everywhere (a non-verifiable proposition) and were interested not in theory but in practice.

MEDIEVAL ETHICS

After the fall of the Western Roman Empire between the fifth and sixteenth centuries there was a relative decay in ethical development because the scientific dimension evaporated from religious dogmatic philosophy. It does not mean that ethics as a *practical* discipline was degraded. Rather, Christian culture brought a significant improvement in practical ethics compared to the Roman Empire. However, theoretical ethics was dogmatized without much space for independent judgment and the ideology of proof. Catholic ethical thought was aesthetic and very useful practically. It would be highly acknowledged by American pragmatists as a working instrumental philosophical framework.

Medieval ethics was quite intellectually challenging. We may recall *Thomas Aquinas'* (1225–1274) efforts in reconciling Aristotle's metaphysics with Christian dogmas, they were really sophisticated and deep. Another task of Aquinas was to develop a rational persuasion of pagans in the true nature of Christianity (logical proofs of God's existence), and this was a very important step in the direction of rational reasoning. However, it was far from scientific. For example, Aquinas developed a sophisticated concept of laws which was actually a *scholastic variant of Deontology*. He distinguished four types of laws: (1) eternal, (2) natural, (3) human, and (4) divine. The *eternal law* is created by God and determines the development of the entire universe. With the help of this law, God directs all things along the necessary path. A man also belongs to this path if he has an innate ability to desire good and distinguish him from evil. Hence comes the second type of laws—the *natural law*, which logically flows from the eternal law and determines the proper behavior of people. We may see that this natural law corresponds to what we now call ethics and a sort of "intuitivism" because people are born with a natural sense of initial principles that are the source of all other knowledge and cannot be proved. For example, statements like "what exists, exists" or "cannot exist at the same time and not exist at the same time" are intuitively obvious, they are natural principles of the mind. Natural law is arranged in the same way and "good should exist" is the same initial principle. The third type of laws are *human laws*—the rules that society creates in order to protect natural law. Human laws imply a system of punishments for violations of natural laws, but since human laws are written by people, they can contain mistakes and turn out to be unfair. An unjust law is wrong and it can and must be broken. The fourth, *divine* laws, are also derived from eternal law but are discovered by a spiritual practice or revelation and written in the sacred texts (in the Old Testament based on fear and in the New Testament based on love). This is an elegant and quite a logical framework but it is not scientific and has a dogmatic foundation which puts its further theoretical development into chains.

SKEPTICISM

Methodological reconstruction of moral philosophy became possible with slow development of scientific method which in its first phase was *skepticism*—an attempt at questioning the correctness of religious dogmas.

The first representatives of skepticism appeared among Islamic theologians. Persian theologian and philosopher *Al-Ghazali* (c. 1058–1111) wanted to challenge ancient thought (first of all—Aristotle) on the basis of rational criticism. For example, he questioned the connection between cause and consequence and claimed that we cannot be sure in this connection even if we observe two phenomena one after another. Another step to rationalist reconstruction of ethics was made by *Mu'tazilites*—a school of theology that flourished in the cities of Basra and Baghdad during the eighth to tenth centuries. They tried to rethink the nature of good and evil from a rational point of view. They claimed that man should try to distinguish good from bad by reason only and he will be rewarded in his future life in accordance with these decisions.

In Europe skepticism became active in the sixteenth to seventeenth centuries. Philosophy was still dominated by scholastic thought but some theologian thinkers started calling, step by step, for a better grounded foundation of knowledge. Many of them raised correct skeptical questions but this investigation often ended with a fideistic conclusion that human abilities are limited and faith should compensate for weakness of reason.

Portuguese and French philosopher *Francisco Sanches* (c. 1550–1623) wrote a piece "That Nothing Is Known" (1581) where he tries to prove that science as finding causes of natural events is impossible because we can never find the ultimate cause, and that all logical knowledge is circular and does not bring us new information. People can generate some limited imperfect knowledge but this requires careful experimental learning. However, Sanches believed that "the answer to moral questions, for example, will be crucially influenced by one's religious conviction" (Caluori 2007, p. 40).

French philosopher *Michel Montaigne* (1533–1592) criticized human readiness to take many things for granted which he understood as some kind of a natural disease of humans. For example, people often think that animals cannot think. But "when I play with my cat, who knows whether I do not make her more sport than she makes me?" Montaigne tried to be skeptical to any traditional truths (his famous "What do I know?"), and ended his inquiry with a quite reasonable conclusion.

French physicist, astronomer and priest *Pierre Gassendi* (1592–1655) also believed that human reason is capable of generating knowledge about many things based on careful observations, but some phenomena will inevitably remain beyond human reasoning, e.g. God's providence. The third part of his *Syntagma philosophicum* ("Philosophical Treatise"), published posthumously in 1658, was devoted to ethics. Gassendi was an admirer of Epicurean ethics but believed that it should be reconciled with Scripture.

BACON AND DESCARTES

The first significant contribution to the development of a scientific method was made by Francis Bacon and Rene Descartes. How did they understand its application to moral philosophy?

The British philosopher *Francis Bacon* (1561–1626) laid down the principles of inductive research and so may be recognized as one of the greatest representatives of empiricism. In his *Great Instauration* project Bacon suggested a plan for building a new general system of sciences all of which should be coherent and built on the same principles. It was an ambitious and incredibly large task, and Bacon assumed that it should be performed collectively by many scholars. So, *Great Instauration* remained unfinished. Unfortunately, its sections about moral philosophy do not constitute a systematic framework and do not offer any new methodological ideas that could stimulate development of a more scientific moral theory. First, as did many scholars before him, Bacon distinguished personal moral philosophy and social moral philosophy but made them more independent of each other[1] (e.g. in contrast to Aristotle who though that ethics and politics significantly overlap). Second, Bacon believed that knowledge about good and evil are given to people by Christianity (like subordination of private to public interests, or value of charity) and people should take them for granted which also was more a scholastic than scientific approach. Bacon thought sciences like psychology may help people to improve their character to come closer to an ideal virtue, but his contribution to normative ethics was limited. His thought about ethics were interesting and thought provoking—e.g. read "Bacon's moral philosophy" by Box (1996) for a careful interpretation—but they were not useful in rebuilding ethics as a science. Bacon was interested in building a typology of various types of ethical knowledge but his ethical analysis represented polemics with ancient authors and was a variant of virtue ethics. We will not find any sign of application of his new scientific method or any new methodological innovation which may lead to a progress in this discipline.

Almost at the same time a similar methodological work was conducted by a French philosopher and mathematician *Rene Descartes* (1596–1650) who also is accounted as a co-father of modern philosophy or science. Descartes started with the same deep skepticism in all human knowledge and was very optimistic about the possibility of rebuilding it from scratch. Descartes believed that all parts of philosophy including ethics should be reconstructed on the basis of his method. He claimed that the ancient moral philosophy (e.g. Aristotelian) was nicely designed but that it obviously lacked sound rational foundation.

> Above all I delighted in mathematics, because of the certainty and self-evidence of its reasonings. But I did not yet notice its real use; and since I thought it was of service only in the mechanical arts, I was surprised that nothing more exalted had been built upon such firm and solid foundations. On the other hand, I compared the moral writings of the ancient pagans to very proud and magnificent palaces built only on sand and mud. They extol the virtues, and make them appear more estimable than anything else in the world; but they do not adequately explain how to recognize a virtue, and often what they call by this fine name is nothing but a case of callousness, or vanity, or desperation, or parricide. (*The Philosophical Writings of Descartes*, p. 114)

Therefore ethics should be rebuilt from scratch and should be just one branch in the tree of sciences.

> Thus the whole philosophy is like a tree. The roots are metaphysics, the trunk is physics, and the branches emerging from the trunk are all the other sciences, which may be reduced to three principal ones, namely medicine, mechanics and morals. By 'morals' I understand the highest and most perfect moral system, which presupposes a complete knowledge of the other sciences and is the ultimate level of wisdom. (*The Philosophical Writings of Descartes*, p. 186)

However, it remained only as a plan. As the first efforts of Descartes were devoted to the roots and the trunk of this tree, he understood that he could not have an opportunity to work seriously on a scientific approach to moral philosophy. Therefore he rationally chose for himself a second best option—to develop a "provisional moral code" on the basis of available moral doctrines which seemed to him wise. He describes this choice in Part 3 of his "Discourse of Method": (1) to obey the laws and customs of my country, (2) to be firm and decisive in my actions when decision is made, (3) to master myself rather than the fortune, and (4) to choose the occupation where I can do my best. As we can see from this code of conduct, it is a synthesis of common sense, Aristotle, and Stoics.

HUGO GROTIUS

An interesting contribution to rational justification of ethics was done by a Dutch legal scientist *Hugo Grotius* (1583–1645), better known as a founder of international law. He was surprised by the unreasonable and voluntarist behavior of nations during conflicts and to minimize the bloodshed in these conflicts he developed a general theory of law which assumed that there are common rules that all nations or people should obey. In 1825 he published *De jure belli ac pacis (On the Law of War and Peace)* which became very popular quite fast and many kings referred to his book in their decisions. Many ideas of this book may be traced to Spanish theologians of the previous century, particularly Francisco de Vitoria and Francisco Suarez, working in the Catholic tradition of natural law. Grotius never distinguished law, politics, and ethics which all represented for him the same norms which people should obey. God's opinions and people's opinion meet on these norms and *even in the absence of God* people would establish the same moral principles.

The natural law would be valid, even if we were to concede, which we can-not concede without the utmost wickedness, that there is no God, or that the affairs of man a of no concern to Him.

The phrase "even in the absence of God" ("etsi deus non daretur" in Latin) became a famous expression which represented one more step to rational justification of ethics. It was also one step to remove influence of religions, because in this framework all religions should agree about the same true natural laws. Like Erasmus, Grotius sought to end the religious disagreement and called for a reconciliation of papacy and Protestants.

THOMAS HOBBES

The really significant progress toward a scientific approach in normative ethics was made by English philosopher *Thomas Hobbes* (1588–1679). He was the first thinker who explicitly built a moral theory based only on rational premises in his famous *Leviathan* (1651). Hobbes lived at the very same time as Descartes although the influence of the latter on Hobbes is not clear.[2] Hobbes had an obvious intention to build a scientific approach to political theory. He was also irritated by the scholastic philosophy of his time which he evaluated as an "insignificant" attempt to merge Christian religion and Aristotle's work. At the same time he was impressed by math-ematics and especially geometry. Finn (2006, p. 52) believes that the geo-metrical method of Hobbes manifested itself most obviously in his explanation of natural laws. Therefore, his answer to scholastic philosophy was an attempt to build a reason-based approach to philosophy. Interestingly, that for some reason Hobbes did not like much experimen-tal knowledge. He was a great admirer of deductive analysis and believed that the major work in building science may be done without experiments and other empirical tools.

His approach in *Leviathan* has strikingly many elements of scientific approach to ethics: accurate definitions, model of man, the idea of agree-ment. First, Hobbes pays a lot of attention to *definitions*. As he writes, even the smartest people may be hopelessly restricted by poor definitions like a bird which fled into the house through the chimney. The first chap-ters of *Leviathan* are full of definitions and bring to mind a glossary. Although not all of these definitions are very accurate, the very intention to start with accurate terminology should be recognized as a very produc-tive principle for philosophy and social science. Following this approach,

Hobbes provided a definition of *good* as a *subjective attitude of a particular person* which exactly fits the scientific approach. For Hobbes, there is no absolute good or evil taken from the nature of the objects, but only individual choices.

> But whatsoever is the object of any man's appetite or desire, that is it which he for his part calleth *good*: and the object of his hate and aversion, *evil*, and of his contempt, *vile* and *inconsiderable*. For these words of good, evil, and contemptible, are ever used with relation to the person that useth them: there being nothing simply and absolutely so; nor any common rule of good and evil, to be taken from the nature of the objects themselves; but from the person of the man... (Hobbes 1839, vol. 4, p. 41)

Second, Hobbes begins his theory with exploration of a *model of man* in the first chapters of *Leviathan* with all his emotions and cognitive characteristics. This is also a very reasonable step because if one wants to build a scientific theory of people's behavior it is necessary first to explain the nature of man's behavior.

Third, Hobbes adheres to *rational choice theory of norms*. As there are no absolute good or evil but only subjective choices, the common moral norms should be also a result of collective subjective choices. To prove this idea one should demonstrate that all people may agree about the same moral norms. Hobbes provides such a proof in the form of his variant of *natural rights theory*. However, this theory contains some unproved propositions. Let us examine it in detail.

Hobbes starts with the idea that all people are equal from birth that is why nobody has more rights than others.

> Nature hath made men so equal, in the faculties of the body, and mind; as that though there be found one man sometimes manifestly stronger in body, or of quicker mind than another; yet when all is reckoned together, the difference between man, and man, is not so considerable, as that one man can thereupon claim to himself any benefit, to which another may not pretend, as well as he. (p. 110)

This proposition is not correct. It would be more accurate to say "nobody has any rights given by nature," but we cannot say "everyone has equal rights" without specifying what these "equal rights" mean.

Hobbes agrees that people actually have different mental and physical capabilities from birth but suggests that these differences are insignificant and we may approximately say that they have equal natural rights. This proposition also seems to be based on a wrong premise. If some people had ten times quicker minds or stronger arms than others, is it a good moral justification for giving them more "natural" rights (as it implicitly follows from Hobbes' argumentation)? If yes, we will arrive at a discriminatory ethical theory leading to some sort of racism, sexism, or elitism.

Later in the text Hobbes gives one more explanation that may be used instead of mental or physical similarity—he points at theoretical possibility that any person can be killed by others, so everyone is *equal in "potential mortality."* However, the theoretical possibility that everyone may be killed by others also *cannot* be a justification of equal natural rights. It is a good argument that can explain why a wise rational strategy for any person, even for very strong one, would be not to abuse this power because there is theoretical possibility that one will lose one's power in the future and may suffer from the revenge of others. This is a very good argument for *rational choice* of norms of equality. It is impossible to derive moral norms from facts like: (1) absence of natural rights, (2) similarity of people's capabilities, and (3) mortality of all people.

Hobbes does use "rational choice" approach when he describes his "war of all against all" framework. The possibility of being killed by others leads to *rational lack of trust* between people. Why it is rational to expect that some people may want to kill you? Hobbes names three causes: competition between people, desire to defend one from others, and glory. These expectations lead to "war of all against all." Here Hobbes makes another interesting claim that there is *nothing unjust in this war.*

> To this war of every man, against every man, this also is consequent; that nothing can be unjust. The notions of right and wrong, justice and injustice have there no place. Where there is no common power, there is no law: where no law, no injustice. Force, and fraud, are in war the two cardinal virtues. Justice, and injustice are none of the faculties neither of the body, nor mind. (p. 115)

This is a puzzling statement. First, there is a confusion of *legal* and *moral* here. Yes, there is no explicit agreement about rights and laws between people, so killing in that situation cannot be illegal. However, *why is killing in that war moral?* If we define a moral thing as "something that people want to exist" and ask these people after the war is over and a political order is established if they wanted this war to exist, the rational answer will be negative. Moreover, even at this war stage we can expect an equilibrium with implicit contracts when two competing actors can reach a peaceful equilibrium without any explicit or formal agreement if they understand that their payoffs will be higher in that situation (e.g. a peace under "mutual assured destruction" doctrine). So, we cannot say that everything is moral in this war.

Therefore, as we see, Hobbes makes some theoretical mistakes which could be avoided if he more consistently followed the methodological principles declared by himself. He argued for more accurate definitions but the definition of "right" and the definition of the hypothetical process which leads to "agreement" remained underspecified or unexplained, therefore leading to mistakes. It is like a geometer ending with errors based on some unspecified conditions or axioms.

After this Hobbes writes that every man has a natural right (*jus naturale*) to live and do what he wants, but there is a natural law (*lex naturalis*) restricting this liberty and forbidding one from committing suicide. Again, there is no good proof of this thesis. The unclear moment is why people need their lives? Why is life something valuable for them? Hobbes does not answer this question and this leaves his conclusion about a natural law forbidding suicide unproved.

Then Hobbes declares a modification of his war model. The first best choice for everyone is not to wage war but *to avoid it.*

And consequently it is a precept, or general rule of reason, that every man, ought to endeavour peace, as far as he has hope of obtaining it; and when he cannot obtain it, that he may seek, and use, all helps, and advantages of war. The first branch of which rule, containeth the first, and fundamental law of nature; which is, to seek peace, and follow it. The second, the sum of the right of nature; which is, by all means we can, to defend ourselves. (p. 117)

After this Hobbes adds:

From this fundamental law of nature, by which men are commanded to endeavour peace, is derived this second law; *that a man be willing, when others are so too, as far-forth, as for peace, and defence of himself he shall think it necessary, to lay down this right to all things; and be contented with so much liberty against other men, as he would allow other men against himself.* For as long as every man holdeth this right, of doing anything he liketh; so long are all men in the condition of war. But if other men will not lay down their right, as well as he; then there is no reason for anyone to divest himself of his: for that were to expose himself to prey, which no man is bound to, rather than to dispose himself to peace. This is that law of the Gospel; *whatsoever you require that others should do to you, that do ye to them.* (pp. 177–178)

Therefore, everyone has the *natural right* to do everything one needs to save one's life, but there is the *first natural law* to avoid war and to seek peace. The *second natural law* is followed from the first—one needs to voluntarily restrict one's rights for some actions which are necessary for peace and enjoy the same restrictions from others. Here Hobbes explicitly ends with Golden Rule and explains it as a rational choice, i.e. maximization of welfare in the situation of reciprocity. This is a variant of rational choice Deontology—a man will support norms which will increase his well-being. If a man violates these norms it is very non-rational thing because other people will never trust this man in the future and will exclude him from moral laws of the society.

After this Hobbes derives several other natural laws (to fulfill promises, to forgive any damage, to revenge only if this improves the future, not to offend anyone, no privileges, and others). These natural laws should be obeyed *in foro interno*, i.e. one should sincerely want them to exist, and not *in foro externo* (enforcement by the state). The science about natural laws is the true moral philosophy.

And the science of [the laws of nature] is the true and only moral philosophy. For moral philosophy is nothing else but the science of what is *good*, and *evil*, in the conversation, and society of mankind. *Good*, and *evil*, are names that signify our appetites, and aversions; which in different tempers, customs, and doctrines of men, are different: and divers men, differ not only in their judgment, on the senses of what is pleasant, and unpleasant to the taste, smell, hearing, touch, and sight; but also of what is conformable, or disagreeable to reason, in the actions of common life. (p. 146)

Hobbes suggests that study of virtues essentially deals with the same laws. Writers on virtues usually do not understand why virtues are virtues, believing that moderateness is good as such but actually all their virtues are good only because they lead to a peaceful and comfortable life.

As we see from this survey Hobbes developed almost all elements of the scientific approach to ethics: (1) definitions, (2) subjective individual rational choice, (3) agreement about moral norms, and (4) neutrality (an implicit Rawlsian justice). Besides this he claimed that only this approach is a true scientific moral theory.

JOHN LOCKE

John Locke (1632–1704) was an English philosopher and physician. Being under the influence of Descartes he put a lot of effort into improving a scientific method. Locke was an early proponent of empiricism. He rejected the idea of Descartes about in-born notions and suggested that the mind of a human newborn is *tabula rasa*, i.e. absolutely clean. All knowledge is generated by experience. However, Locke suggested that moral philosophy may be constructed similar to mathematics. This idea is expressed in Locke's main treatise on epistemology, *Essay on Human Understanding* (1689). Book 4 "On Knowledge and Opinion" of *Essay* is devoted to the nature of knowledge and emphasizes that knowledge is essentially ideas nested in our minds. However, in chapter 4 "Of the Reality of Knowledge" in this book he claims that ideas in our head should agree or conform with reality, otherwise there will be little value to them and the ideas of sober clever educated man will have the same value as the dreams of an insane, drunk, uneducated man. First, Locke claims that mathematical knowledge is real because when real objects correspond to qualities of mathematical figures they should have the same qualities (e.g. any real triangle should have three angles equal to 180 degrees). Then Locke suddenly comes to ethics and also claims that *moral knowledge may be real as a mathematical one.*

And hence it follows that moral knowledge is as capable of real certainty, as mathematics. For certainty being but the perception of the agreement or disagreement of our ideas; and demonstration nothing but the perception of such agreement, by the intervention of other ideas, or mediums; our moral ideas, as well as mathematical, being archetypes themselves, and so adequate and complete ideas; all the agreement or disagreement, which we shall find in them, will produce real knowledge, as well as in mathematical figures. (Locke 1824, vol. 2, p. 129)

Unfortunately, there is no further development of this methodological claim in the *Essay*, so it remains only a belief as it was in case of Descartes. However, in the main political work of John Locke *Two Treatises on Government* (1689) there is an example of such an approach—a variant of natural rights theory. *Treatises* were wrote as a reaction to a divine theory of monarchy suggested by Robert Filmer (?–1653) in his work *The Necessity of the Absolute Power of all Kings* (1648). The main idea of Filmer was that no one is born free and the power of the king is of a divine origin.

In the first treatise Lock criticizes Filmer and in the second suggests his own explanation of rights based on reason.

> ...there being nothing more evident, than that creatures of the same species and rank, promiscuously born to all the same advantages of nature, and the use of the same faculties, should also be equal one amongst another without subordination or subjection... (Locke 1824, vol. 4, p. 339)
>
> The state of nature has a law of nature to govern it, which obliges every one: and reason, which is that law, teaches all mankind, who will but consult it, that being all equal and independent, no one ought to harm another in his life, health, liberty, or possessions... (p. 341)

Here Locke makes the same mistake as Hobbes. We can say that in the state of nature no one has any right—this is the only fact of equality. We cannot say that everyone has the natural right to live. This is a logical mistake. The proposition *"being all equal and independent, no one ought to harm another in his life, health, liberty, or possessions"* is unproven. To prove it we need every person to *accept* it as a rational defense against corresponding risks and a good institutional environment for economic growth and prosperity.

The next claim of Locke was that "every man hath a right to punish the offender, and be executioner of the law of nature" (p. 342) but it is also without proof. It can be proved on the basis of rational agreement theory but Locke does not use one.

Similarly, Locke suggests that property rights emanate from labor spent to produce something, but again it should be an agreement of people and cannot be a matter of fact.

> Though the earth, and all inferior creatures, be common to all men, yet every man has a property in his own person: this nobody has any right to but himself. The labour of his body, and the work of his hands, we may say, are properly his. Whatsoever then he removes out of the state that nature hath provided, and left it in, he hath mixed his labour with, and joined to it something that is his own, and thereby makes it his property. (Locke 1824, vol. 4, pp. 353–354)

As we see Locke and Hobbes come very close to scientific moral theory, but some of their propositions lacked proper argumentation. They implicitly suggested that some "values" directly follow from "facts" but there should be a subjective individual choice and collective agreement between the former and the latter.

SHAFTESBURY, HUTCHESON AND SMITH

After Hobbes and Locke provided their variants of rational choice moral theory which viewed moral norms as a result of collective agreement, some writers were dissatisfied. Many of them shared an ideology of deism, i.e. although they denied direct interference of God in the world, they prefer to think that the world and man have some innate goodness. They wanted to demonstrate that morality indeed has some real or objective character. So these writers decided to focus on natural moral feelings of people.

The first proponent of this approach was an English philosopher Anthony Ashley Cooper, *the Third Earl of Shaftesbury* (1671–1713). His family was close to John Locke who made some impact on the education of young Anthony. However, this influence did not prevent Shaftesbury from becoming unhappy with the influence of Locke and Hobbes on moral philosophy. Shaftesbury tried to show that actually every man has a special natural capability—*moral sense*—which has the same nature as a sense of beauty. This moral sense means ability to admire the beauty of virtuous behavior as sense of beauty helps to experience the beauty of painting. It was an attempt to build a synthesis of aesthetics and ethics which is highly recognized by the historians of thought. The writings of Shaftesbury did not look like theorizing but more like literature, but then he was aiming to persuade the nobility and not scholars.

The approach of Shaftesbury was developed further by *Francis Hutcheson* (1694–1746) a professor of Moral Philosophy at the University of Glasgow. He published a treatise *An Inquiry into the Original of Our Ideas of Beauty and Virtue»* (1725) which also had two parts: on aesthetics and on ethics. Hutcheson also explained both aesthetic and ethical behavior of people by *internal senses*—capabilities of a person to feel good or bad when one is observing beautiful or virtuous things. For Hutcheson there are two types of good: *natural good* (like food or drinks which bring pleasure to the person) and *moral good* (pure altruistic behavior, when a man helps others not expecting a future reward but because of "love of others"). Capability to feel this moral goodness represents *internal moral sense* of man. Hutcheson recognized three types of this moral sense: *public sense* (be pleased at the happiness of others), *moral sense* (be pleased when acting in virtue), and *sense of honor* (be pleased when your good behavior is acknowledged by others). Hutcheson suggests that this instinctive behavior leads people to a better result that their conscious choice. Internal senses were designed by our Creator and help us to make quickly right decisions when our reason can make a mistake. Hutcheson admits that sometimes feelings may push people to commit bad actions, but claims that generally feelings of moral goodness prevail and lead mankind to a better outcome. Here Hutcheson anticipates some ideas of the evolutionary model of man which also suggests that some instincts ("moral senses") help to compensate weaknesses in human reason.

However, what if different people have *different* feelings about altruistic behavior? How to decide who is more ethical? Hutcheson admits that moral sense may give people different positive rewards but assumes that this difference is insignificant, and moral sense cannot be fundamentally wrong.

How should a morally good man compare different actions and choose the best one? Here Hutcheson comes with a *utilitarian idea*—maximizing net total happiness of all people who are influenced by this decision—using the famous phrase "the greatest happiness for the greatest number."

> In comparing the moral Qualitys of Actions, in order to regulate our Election among various Actions propos'd, or to find which of them has the greatest moral Excellency, we are led by our moral Sense of Virtue to judge thus; that in equal Degrees of Happiness, expected to proceed from the Action, the Virtue is in proportion to the Number of Persons to whom the Happiness shall extend; (and here the Dignity, or moral Importance of Persons, may compensate Numbers) and in equal Numbers, the Virtue is as the Quantity of the Happiness, or natural Good; or that the Virtue is in a compound Ratio of the Quantity of Good, and Number of Enjoyers. In the same manner, the moral Evil, or Vice, is as the Degree of Misery, and Number of Sufferers; so that, that Action is best, which procures the greatest Happiness for the greatest Numbers; and that, worst, which, in like manner, occasions Misery. (*Inquiry concerning Moral Good and Evil*, sect. 3, VIII)

Hutcheson explicitly suggests that if an increase in Happiness compensates the loss of happiness by some people the action is morally good, but not in all cases. If a small increase of happiness of many people is received at the cost of enormous sufferings of a few people, this action is not morally good. This is an extremely important principle which actually lifts much later criticism of Utilitarianism. Hutcheson does not provide an explicit proof of this proposition but he probably could have said that it is supported by the moral sense.

Hutcheson also suggests his variant of moral goodness computation which was also an anticipation of future felicitous calculus offered later by

Bentham. However, in Hutcheson's case the computation is focused on measuring not consequences but moral goodness and abilities of actors. He says that the amount of moral good a person can produce depends on two variables: (1) the degree of one's altruism and (2) one's capabilities to makes things happen.

> The moral Importance of any Agent, or the Quantity of publick Good produc'd by him, is in a compound Ratio of his Benevolence and Abilitys: or (by substituting the initial Letters for the Words, as M—Moment of Good, and μ—Moment of Evil) M = B × A. (*Inquiry concerning Moral Good and Evil*, sect. 3, XI)

This is a strange statement for several reasons. First, earlier Hutcheson stated that the degree of altruism (moral sense) is almost the same for all people, but now it becomes a significant variable. Second, the quantity of public good which a person produces also depends on many other factors (e.g. social position of the actor, economic and political situation, and many others). Probably, Hutcheson implicitly makes a *ceteris paribus* assumption but still the question remains why we need this type of calculation of "quantity of public good"?

Hutcheson also made an important thesis that his moral theory is a universal theory, i.e. all people should agree that this foundation of morality is true. This thesis may be proved by the fact that in various societies people may have different opinions about natural good (e.g. they may value some pleasures more than others) but in all societies any action is evaluated on the basis of its moral goodness, i.e. how it increases the happiness of other people.

As we have seen, Hutcheson made two important contributions to the development of the objective or scientific theory of morality: the evolutionary model of man with his theory of senses and the idea of the universal moral theory which everyone should support. The limitation of his approach is the confusion between positive and normative analysis. An attempt to remove this confusion will be made by one of his followers who is discussed in the next section.

DAVID HUME

Although some empiricists (e.g. Locke) assumed the possibility of scientific moral knowledge, a famous representative of the empiricist camp—a Scottish philosopher *David Hume* (1711–1776)—expressed a negative opinion on the issue. His main philosophical work *A Treatise of Human Nature* (1739) was devoted mostly to possibility of human knowledge and the basic functioning of human mind. In the first book of the *Treatise* Hume makes a principal distinction between two types of knowledge—*impressions* (sensations and feelings) and *ideas* (abstract concepts of any other things including the ideas of impressions). Based on this framework he builds radical criticism of the ability to know casual relationships, because only *facts* may be observed but not the *casual connections* between them. The latter may be only assumed by reason but can be never observed as such by sensations, so we can never know them for sure. It was a very radical claim because it added much skepticism to any scientific theory.

In the third book of the *Treatise* which is called *Of Morals* Hume developed a similarly radical approach to moral knowledge. In the very beginning he puts the main question: "Whether it is by means of our ideas or impressions we distinguish between vice and virtue, and pronounce an action blamable or praiseworthy" (Book 3, page 1)? He starts with criticizing those who believes that morality may be derived by reason and may be the same for every person. Instead, Hume suggests that ideas of good and evil are based on our *passions*. First, it is passions that create positive and negative feelings in our mind. When we see something we like, we have positive feelings and we call it good. There is no place for reason in this process; our moral propositions are totally based on passions. Second, only moral ideas in our mind can generate passions which can make us move, and this incentive cannot be created by reason. Reason can discover that some objects may bring positive feelings to the person, but *reason cannot create these feelings*, because they are created only by passions. That is why morality cannot be derived from reason. Let us provide several citations of Hume's explanation of this position because Hume's influence on further development of moral philosophy was enormous and it is useful to have a fuller account of his key arguments.

> But can there be any difficulty in proving, that vice and virtue are not matters of fact, whose existence we can infer by reason? Take any action allow'd to be vicious: Wilful murder, for instance. Examine it in all lights, and see if you can find that matter of fact, or real existence, which you call vice. In which-ever way you take it, you find only certain passions, motives, volitions and thoughts. There is no other matter of fact in the case. The vice entirely escapes you, as long as you consider the object. You never can find it, till you turn your reflection into your own breast, and find a sentiment of

disapprobation, which arises in you, towards this action. Here is a matter of fact; but `tis the object of feeling, not of reason. It lies in yourself, not in the object. So that when you pronounce any action or character to be vicious, you mean nothing, but that from the constitution of your nature you have a feeling or sentiment of blame from the contemplation of it. Vice and virtue, therefore, may be compar'd to sounds, colours, heat and cold, which, according to modern philosophy, are not qualities in objects, but perceptions in the mind. (*A Treatise of Human Nature*, Book III, Part I, Section I)

This framework looks logical but this is a confusion of normative and positive ethics. A model of shaping moral judgments under influence of emotions is a positive ethics analysis. This model does not prove impossibility of normative ethics based on rational choice under full control of emotions.

Interestingly, Hume understood two different kind of propositions—positive and normative—and even claimed the impossibility of deriving normative propositions from positive ones.

In every system of morality, which I have hitherto met with, I have always remarked, that the author proceeds for some time in the ordinary way of reasoning, and establishes the being of a God, or makes observations concerning human affairs; when of a sudden I am surprised to find, that instead of the usual copulations of propositions, is, and is not, I meet with no proposition that is not connected with an ought, or an ought not. This change is imperceptible; but is, however, of the last consequence. For as this ought, or ought not, expresses some new relation or affirmation, 'tis necessary that it should be observed and explained; and at the same time that a reason should be given, for what seems altogether inconceivable, how this new relation can be a deduction from others, which are entirely different from it. But as authors do not commonly use this precaution, I shall presume to recommend it to the readers; and am persuaded, that this small attention would subvert all the vulgar systems of morality, and let us see, that the distinction of vice and virtue is not founded merely on the relations of objects, nor is perceived by reason.

This methodological rule was later called *is-ought* problem and supported by the majority of philosophers. Black (1964) called this problem Hume's Guillotine; R.M. Hare (1952) called it Hume's Law. This rule looks very logical but again everything depends on the definitions. If Hume had defined moral science as a search of subjective moral truth, he would come to the opposite conclusion. Actually, he was very close to this result because he assumed that all moral judgments are generated in our "own breast" but he focused on the role of emotions and neglected rational choice.

This thesis is well proved by the further content of *Treatise*. Part II of Book III "*Of Morals*" is devoted to justice, and here Hume develops argumentation which is very similar to natural rights theorists and evolutionary theory of emotions. Hume writes that the most basic emotion of humans is egoism. However, human beings are weak and cannot provide themselves all necessary goods alone. Beside this, human beings may be aggressive to each other. However, human beings learn and experiment and soon understand that being aggressive and exploitative to each other is not very wise and therefore decide to refrain from the desire to rob each other. So, they gradually develop feelings for common interests and justice. Essentially, this is a *natural selection explanation of emotions*. Again, it makes sense to provide here several quotes from Hume to demonstrate his approach to this issue.

> ....a convention entered into by all the members of the society to bestow stability on the possession of those external goods, and leave everyone in the peaceable enjoyment of what he may acquire by his fortune and industry. By this means, everyone knows what he may safely possess....
>
> ...Two men, who pull the oars of a boat, do it by an agreement or convention, though they have never given promises to each other. Nor is the rule concerning the stability of possession the less derived from human conventions, that it arises gradually, and acquires force by a slow progression, and by our repeated experience of the inconveniences of transgressing it... In like manner are languages gradually established by human conventions without any promise. In like manner do gold and silver become the common measures of exchange...
>
> I have already observed, that justice takes its rise from human conventions; and that these are intended as a remedy to some inconveniences, which proceed from the concurrence of certain qualities of the human mind with the situation of external objects. The qualities of the mind are selfishness and limited generosity... (*A Treatise of Human Nature*, Book III, Part I, Section II)

Interestingly, Hume notes that if all people were absolute altruists (= have strong moral sense in Hutcheson's terms) the concept of justice would lose its meaning, because justice is only necessary to restrict behavior of egoists.

As we see from this citation, Hume offers a theory of justice which is essentially another variant of social contract theory (developed earlier by Hobbes and Locke) and an evolutionary model of man. Surprisingly, this theory of justice in Section II *contradicts* Hume's theory that morality cannot be derived by reason in Section I, and the problem is not Hume's logical mistake in any of these theories, but just definitions. If Hume defined moral theory as study of personal judgments about goods and bads and social agreement about goods and bads, both parts of his moral theory would be reconciled and the whole framework would be very close to the scientific variant of ethics described in this book.

An interesting theory that partly stems from non-naturalism but at the same time admits existence of moral truth is *intuitionism*. It holds that basic moral propositions are *self-evident* for a person, so they do not need to be proved. Early intuitionists were John Balguy, Ralph Cudworth, and Samuel Clarke who also tried to criticize Thomas Hobbes. Later, this approach was developed by *Richard Price* (1723–1791)—a minister of a Unitarian church who wrote on various social issues. In 1758 he delivered a book *The Review of the Principal Questions in Morals* to argue against the theory of moral senses of F. Hutcheson. In the beginning of the book he says that there are some actions that we all feel ourselves irresistibly determined to approve, and others to disapprove, and then asks the question: "What is the power within us that determines us to make these judgments?" There might be two powers—*immediate understanding* and *immediate feelings*. Price claims that it is immediate understanding because good and bad is something objective which may be understood. Immediate feelings are about internal phenomena so they can vary and cannot be a foundation for morals (that is why Hutcheson was wrong). At the same time, immediate understanding does not require any argumentation, because ideas of right and wrong are *simple ideas* and they are understood by immediate perception of human mind. It is impossible to define them through their synonyms (like "right" means "correct"). Similarly, there are some ends which are ultimately approved so we do not need other ends to approve them as a means and get these ends by immediate understanding.

An interesting development of the theory of moral senses was made by *Adam Smith* (1723–1790), who was a student of Hutcheson and Hume. Although Smith is known mostly by his famous treatise in economic theory *Wealth of Nations* (1776), his career began in the area of ethics. In 1752 Smith took the position of professor of moral philosophy and after several years of lecturing in this subject he summarized them in the book *Theory of Moral Sentiments* (1759). What contribution to ethics was made by the famous economist? If *Wealth of Nations* was a large collection of observations and explanations of how market functions, *Theory of Moral Sentiments* was a large collection of observations and explanations of how people's emotions operate in social interaction. Essentially it was a long essay in descriptive psychology with some elements of normative ethics. The main purpose of the author was to describe and explain various moral feelings experienced by people and their functions in the society, that is why from time to time he switches to analysis of social consequences and after this sometimes makes normative implications. Methodologically this was done in a very spontaneous manner so *Theory of Moral Sentiments* is an interweaving of positive and normative statements typical for all early moral texts like *Nicomachean Ethics*. Smith mostly repeats the ideas of his predecessors although researchers claim that he tried to reinterpret them and add something new (see Raphael 2007).

One of these ideas was the *impartial observer*. It was used by Hutcheson and Hume in their works but in the context of evaluating the behavior of other people. For example, sense of beauty in Hutcheson's framework is the ability to see the beauty of benevolent behavior when you are looking at it from aside, *not being interested* in it. Smith used this idea when he described the self-evaluation of agent's decisions. Theoretically, it could be an excellent criterion of moral evaluation which may compete with Golden Rule or Categorical Imperative, but Smith conceptualized it more as a positive than normative theory (it describes how people make moral evaluation).

Whenever I try to examine my own conduct—whenever I try to pass sentence on it, and either approve or condemn it—it's obvious that I divide myself into two persons (so to speak), and that in my role as examiner and judge I represent a different character from that of myself as the person whose conduct is examined and judged. One is the spectator, whose sentiments concerning my own conduct I try to enter into by placing myself in his situation and considering how it would appear to me when seen from that particular point of view. The other is the agent, the person whom I properly call 'myself', the person about whose conduct I as spectator was trying to form some opinion. The first is the judge, the second the person judged. (Theory, Part III, Chapter 1, paragraph 8)

It was possible to make a normative theory from this idea but it would be necessary to answer two questions: (1) why is it ethical to make decisions on the basis of impartial spectator criterion? and (2) what principles does the impartial spectator use to evaluate actions?

Reading *Theory* we can make one more important observation which refutes many later accusations against Adam Smith in apology of selfish behavior. Actually, Smith believed that the first best situation is when people help each other on the basis of mutual sympathy, but if this is impossible the second best is the interaction of selfish people who agree to cooperate through the market system. The third variant is the society of selfish people who hate one another and want to kill each other—this society cannot exist at all.

CLASSIC UTILITARIANISM

Jeremy Bentham (1748–1832) was not an inventor of Utilitarianism, because all ideas were suggested right before his time by various scholars (e.g. Hutcheson). Bentham wrote his first work on moral theory *A Fragment on Government* (1776) to criticize W. Blackstone's *Commentaries on the Laws of England* (1765–1769)—a comprehensive description of the common law in four volumes. Bentham claimed that Blackstone was too conservative, defended obsolete laws and did not understand real principle which should be used to build a legal system. Bentham's fierce criticism was not always fair to Blackstone's real contribution to legal studies and his suggested reforms were not always realistic (Posner 1976), but here we are interested more in the moral theory used by Bentham as a foundation for his legal reforms. It was the famous "principle of utility" and Utilitarianism.

From the very beginning of the *Fragment* it becomes clear that Bentham makes a call to rebuild moral theory on a new foundation. He suggested that there were significant "discoveries" in the natural world during the last century but a similar significant discovery in the moral world performed by several authors remained unfairly unnoticed. This discovery was the "principle of greatest happiness of greatest number" or "principle of utility." However Bentham did not follow (and probably did not understood) the scientific method in all its aspects, e.g. the need for providing accurate proofs of every deductive or inductive proposition. Although he severely criticized his opponents for suggesting unproved nonsense, he did not bother himself with accurate proof of his own theory. His theory seemed obvious for himself and it was enough for him to assume that every reasonable person should also think so. As a result, Bentham could not persuade many of his readers who eventually decided to reject Utilitarianism. It was a sad consequence and Bentham would be really unhappy if he saw the future development of moral theory in the next two centuries. We can guess that one of his biggest disappointment would be establishment of three alternative approaches in the moral philosophy—Utilitarianism, Deontology and Virtue Ethics. For Bentham it was a non-sense. He suggested a general framework to moral philosophy with elements of all these approaches but he did not pay attention to proofs and as a result failed to convince everyone that it is a good synthesis.

For example, the first chapter of the *Fragment* represents a discussion of natural law theory. Bentham starts with a criticism of terminology of Blackstone ("state of nature" and "society"), and offers a more accurately defined set of concepts which is obviously a symptom of a more scientific approach to building a theory. But then he tries to reject the "original contract" theory as a "fiction" because no such agreement took place in the past. And even if it was made no one now "ought" to obey this agreement for the sake of this historical origin. Instead, Bentham insists that this contract is remade every day between the government and people who understand that life with order and governance is better than without them.

> But after all, for what reason is it, that men *ought* an original to keep their promises? The moment any intelligible reason is given, it is this: that it is for the *advantage* of society they should keep them; and if they do not, that, as far as *punishment* will go, they should be *made* to keep them. It is for the advantage of the whole number that the promises of each individual should be kept: and, rather than they should not be kept, that such individuals as fail to keep them should be punished. (*Fragment*, p. 159)

Although this may be a rejection of "original contract" theory, it is actually a confirmation of *social contract theory* demonstrating that Bentham essentially suggested a synthesis of all major ideas in moral philosophy.

The next major work of Bentham *An Introduction to the Principles of Morals and Legislation* (1789) represented a more systematic development of a new moral theory and its application to criminal law. Although, Bentham made an attempt to make this theory comprehensive many really important moments of this moral theory remained obscure. First, Bentham distinguished 14 kinds of pleasure and 11 kinds of pain, and suggested several parameters which influence the size of pleasure (length, intensity, sureness, etc.). However, he did not suggest a practical method of measuring pleasure and did not pose a question of how the theory should be applied to practical issues if this method was not found. He listed 54 synonyms to pleasure, and 67 synonyms of pain but all this labor had no more use to normative ethics than linguistic discussions in meta-ethics in the twentieth century (see the next chapter). Second, Bentham suggested that it is permissible to sacrifice the smaller pain of some people for the larger pleasure of others, but he did not prove this thesis and did not pose a question what is a criterion for morally permissible sacrifice. However, it is the problem of this criteria that becomes the mainstay of later criticism of Utilitarian theory together with the problem of measurability. Generally, Bentham was quite careless with providing proof of all what he was saying. His application of "principle of utility" to criminal law in *Principles* was mostly speculative and it is unclear how Bentham was going to seek consent from others who would disagree with his conclusions.

It seems that Bentham failed to not make his theory more scientific because he lacked the idea of science (expressed 150 years before him by Bacon or Descartes) and was not influenced by mathematical methods (like Hobbes). Also it seems that he missed the fundamental *is-ought* problem which was already explained by David Hume (although Bentham read Hume's *Treatise of Human Nature* and even referred to Hume's criticism of original contract theory). It is strange that Bentham himself made no distinction between positive and normative analysis, although he was one step from resolving Hume's guillotine. He did not think that the "principle of utility" requires proof, because it could be used as an axiom in moral theory.

> Is [principle of utility] susceptible of any direct proof? It seems not, because something that is used to prove everything else can't itself be proved; a chain of proofs must start somewhere. To give such a proof is as impossible as it is needless.

Refusal to give proof is a weak option for a moral theory because such a theory may be rejected by anyone who disagrees with this axiom. Bentham could easily say that *this axiom can be proved* by the universal agreement of people. It would be compatible with his claim that those who try to disagree with the principle of utility actually are using the same principle of utility implicitly.

> When a man tries to combat the principle of utility, his reasons are drawn—without his being aware of it—from that very principle itself. If his arguments prove anything, it isn't that the principle is wrong but that he is applying it wrongly. Is it possible for a man to move the earth? Yes; but he must first find out another earth to stand on.

What Bentham wants to say here is that actually all people naturally agree with the principle of utility and it is impossible to think of another foundation of morality. Interestingly Bentham implicitly constructs a sort of Socratic dialogue toward the end of chapter 1, aimed at persuading anyone who disagrees that actually one agrees with the principle of utility.

The last important moral work of Bentham was *Deontology; Or, The Science of Morality in which the Harmony and Co-incidence of Duty and Self-interest, Virtue and Felicity, Prudence and Benevolence, Are Explained, Exemplified and Applied to Business of Life* (1838) which became an even more obvious demonstration of his position described above. In this book Bentham once more declared that there should be a synthesis of various moral traditions on the basis of the "principle of utility." He offers a new name for the discipline of right and wrong actions—Deontology—and suggests that it should be based on the principle of utility.

> The principle, then, on which Deontology is grounded, is the principle of Utility; in other words, that every action is right or wrong, worthy or unworthy, deserving approbation or disapprobation, in proportion to its tendency to contribute to, or to diminish the amount of public happiness. (p. 24)

Bentham wanted to find an objective foundation for morality which would convince everyone instead of dogmatic theories of duties which had no proof. This foundation is the idea of rational choice which is expressed by Bentham through concepts of "interests" and "prudence."

> A man, a moralist, gets into an elbow chair, and pours forth pompous dogmatisms about *duty* and *duties*. Why is he not listened to? Because every man is thinking about *interests* <…>

To place prominently forward the connection between interest and duty in all the concerns of private life, is the object now proposed. The more closely the subject is examined, the more obvious will the agreement between interest and duty appear. All laws which have for their end the happiness of those concerned, endeavour to make that for a man is interest which they proclaim to be his duty. And in the moral field it cannot be a man's duty to do that which it is his interest not to do. (pp. 10–11)

In other words, the principle of utility should be the basis for any deontological theory—for any norms, rights, duties, etc. Moreover, Bentham embedded the concept of virtue in the same framework. Virtue is a trait of character that helps one to maximize one's happiness and includes two capabilities: prudence (= rational choice) and effective benevolence (= enlightened egoism).

And how can their happiness be best provided for by you? How but by the exercise of the virtues of those qualities the union of which is *virtue*? Virtue divides itself into two branches: *prudence* and *effective benevolence*. Prudence has its seat in the understanding. Effective benevolence principally in the affections; those affections which, when intense and strong, become passions. (p. 15)

The first law of nature is to wish our own happiness; and the united voices of prudence and efficient benevolence, add,—seek the happiness of others,—seek your own happiness in the happiness of others. (p. 17)

This is Bentham's version of Golden Rule which means that it is rational for everyone to maximize general happiness of all people, because if everyone makes this choice his or her happiness will be maximized.

Half a century later, Bentham's ideas were refined by *John Stuart Mill* (1806–1873)—the last significant representative of classical political economy, a philosopher of logics and liberty. He was the son of James Mill who was a friend of Bentham and Ricardo, so it is not surprising that John Stuart Mill shared the same values and beliefs with them. However, for Mill it was not a matter of "belief" because he was very interested in developing scientific methods and in 1843 he published *A System of Logic, Ratiocinative and Inductive, Being a Connected View of the Principles of Evidence, and the Methods of Scientific Investigation.* He suggested that laws should be discovered through observation and induction, and required empirical verification. The same scientific approach should be applied to moral philosophy. If we look for a scientific principle in moral philosophy we will find the principle of utility.

> There are not only first principles of Knowledge, but first principles of Conduct. There must be some standard by which to determine the goodness or badness, absolute and comparative, of ends or objects of desire. And whatever that standard is, there can be but one. <…>
> [T]he general principle to which all rules of practice ought to conform, and the test by which they should be tried, is that of conduciveness to the happiness of mankind [...] the promotion of happiness is the ultimate principle of Teleology. (System, VIII: 951)

Bentham's theory was much criticized at that time and in 1861 Mill wrote three articles for a magazine to clarify and defend the principle of utility, published in 1863 as a small book called *Utilitarianism*. In the beginning of this book Mill is surprised by how significant and sustainable disagreement between moral philosophers is and that although the very same ideas have been discussed for two thousand years, there is still no solution which could satisfy everyone. Then he provides his arguments in defense of Utilitarianism where we may find several interesting methodological ideas representing the slow progress of moral philosophy toward the scientific methodology.

First, Mill gets back to the basic definitions and assumptions of moral theory and ascertains that it is difficult to prove the basic assumptions about good. Music is good because it adds utility, but why is utility good? In chapter 1 he makes a hint that this "is not a subject of what is commonly understood by proof" (paragraph 5), but the whole chapter 4 is devoted to the problem of proof of utility principle and suggests that it is *subjective individual choice*. Good is good because people want it, and no more proof is necessary.

> The only proof capable of being given that an object is visible is that people actually see it. The only proof that a sound is audible, is that people hear it: and so of the other sources of our experience. In like manner, I apprehend, the sole evidence it is possible to produce that anything is desirable, is that people do actually desire it. If the end which the utilitarian doctrine proposes to itself were not, in theory and in practice, acknowledged to be an end, nothing could ever convince any person that it was so. (Chapter 4, paragraphs 2–3)

Second, Mill makes a reservation about *conditions* of individual choice. A necessary condition to different variants is knowledge. Therefore, we can make decisions for people who lack knowledge.

> From the verdict of the only competent judges, I apprehend there can be no appeal. On a question which is the best worth having of two pleasures, or which of two modes of existence is the most grateful to the feelings, apart from its moral attributes and from its consequences, the judgment of those who are qualified by knowledge of both, or, if they differ, that of the majority among them, must be admitted as final. (Chapter 2, paragraph 10)

Third, Mill makes an assumption about the necessity of impartiality in making judgments about total utility. Here is the idea of the Impartial Spectator which was suggested by Adam Smith, but is now presented similar to veil of ignorance.

> I must again repeat, what the assailants of Utilitarianism seldom have the justice to acknowledge, that the happiness which forms the utilitarian standard of what is right in conduct, is not the agent's own happiness, but that of all concerned. As between his own happiness and that of others, Utilitarianism requires him to be as strictly impartial as a disinterested and benevolent spectator. (Chapter 2, paragraph 21)

Fourth, Mill believed that there should be an agreement about one true moral philosophy. He carefully examined the arguments of all critics of Utilitarianism and demonstrated that they were actually based on the same utility principle. Correspondingly, there is no difference between Utilitarianism and Deontology because all moral norms of the latter actually support the principle of utility.

> In the golden rule of Jesus of Nazareth, we read the complete spirit of the ethics of utility. To do as you would be done by, and to love your neighbour as yourself, constitute the ideal perfection of utilitarian morality. (Chapter 2, paragraph 21)

Intuitive ethics and Utilitarianism also do not contradict each other.

> It is not necessary, for the present purpose, to decide whether the feeling of duty is innate or implanted. Assuming it to be innate, it is an open question to what objects it naturally attaches itself; for the philosophic supporters of

that theory are now agreed that the intuitive perception is of principles of morality and not of the details. If there be anything innate in the matter, I see no reason why the feeling which is innate should not be that of regard to the pleasures and pains of others. If there is any principle of morals which is intuitively obligatory, I should say it must be that. If so, the intuitive ethics would coincide with the utilitarian, and there would be no further quarrel between them. (Chapter 3, paragraph 7)

Virtue ethics is also compatible with Utilitarianism because virtues are only tools to achieve happiness.

It results from the preceding considerations, that there is in reality nothing desired except happiness. Whatever is desired otherwise than as a means to some end beyond itself, and ultimately to happiness, is desired as itself a part of happiness, and is not desired for itself until it has become so. Those who desire virtue for its own sake, desire it either because the consciousness of it is a pleasure, or because the consciousness of being without it is a pain, or for both reasons united... (Chapter 4, paragraph 8)

IMMANUEL KANT

Immanuel Kant (1724–1804), one of the most influential figures in moral philosophy, suggested a very interesting example of methodology which claimed to achieve the same purpose as a scientific ethics—to produce genuine moral truth. Kant thought that he was conducting a Copernican Revolution both in metaphysics and moral philosophy because his new method of philosophy should be able to answer many questions. His major philosophical book *Critique of Pure Reason* (1781) tried to resolve old debate between a rationalist (Descartes) who believed that all knowledge comes from reason, and an empiricist (Hume) who believed that all knowledge comes from senses. Kant agreed that most knowledge come from senses but suggested that at least some non-tautological knowledge about the world is derived by our mind. He came out with the idea that the human mind creates some basic concepts or structures of human experience (like time and space) and there are at least some synthetic propositions that may be known a priori. Several years later Kant applied the same method to moral philosophy and tried to figure out what moral propositions may be known a priori, i.e. regardless of any particular circumstances of individual choice. He published first a preliminary version of his moral theory as *Groundwork of the Metaphysic of*

Morals (1785), which was followed by a more detailed account in *Critique of Practical Reason* (1788), and later in *Metaphysics of Morals* (1797).

Obviously, Kant's methodology of moral philosophy was a significant step toward a scientific approach to ethics. First, Kant suggested a clear border between positive and normative ethics. He drew an analogy between ethics and physics, both of which have an empirical and a rational part. In case of ethics it is *practical anthropology* (= positive ethics) and *morals* (= normative ethics). Kant was very critical about confusing normative and positive analysis.

> That which mixes these pure principles with empirical ones does not even deserve the name of philosophy. (p. 4)

Second, Kant made an ambitious attempt to build an *objective* moral theory which should be derived by Pure Reason without taking into account any subjective factors and circumstances. He suggested that we should look for foundation of moral laws "a priori simply in concepts of Pure Reason." Practical anthropology can explain how morality of real people evolves but it can say nothing to normative analysis. Moral laws cannot borrow anything from moral anthropology but only can give something to the latter.

> Is it not thought to be of the utmost necessity to work out for once a pure moral philosophy, completely cleansed of everything that may be only empirical and that belongs to anthropology? (*Groundwork*, p. 2)

As a result of this analysis Kant derived an a priori moral norm which is *universal*, i.e. every Pure reason should agree with this norm. Again, this is very consonant to the scientific approach to ethics because Kant admits that there should be unanimous consensus between all people about these moral norms.

> For, that there must be such a philosophy is clear of itself from the common idea of duty and of moral laws. Everyone must grant that a law, if it is to hold morally, that is, as a ground of an obligation, must carry with it absolute necessity. (*Groundwork*, p. 2)

However, some elements in Kantian framework do not fit the scientific approach. First, Pure Reason can make any decision a priori only if it has a criterion of choice. It would be natural to assume that this is *rational choice*, but instead Kant assumes that these decisions are based on *good will*. He explains this concept as follows. If we want to find a moral truth a priori, we should ask if there is anything *unconditionally good*. Many things are good or bad depending on the situation. The only thing which is good in all situations is "good will"—a desire to be good or make a good action. This proposition looks correct but is it not a tautological (analytical) proposition? It says only that "desire to be good is good." Moreover, there is no definition of "good" in the Kantian framework and this is one of its biggest methodological problems. If we do not define "good" how we can make and verify any further propositions on what is good and what is not?

Second, for Kant an action is good *only* if it is made with good will. This action may lead to evil consequences if the actor has lack of knowledge. However, it is still good because the intention was good. This is why Kantian theory is sometimes called a theory of intentions. However, intention and action are not the same. We may have good intentions but treat patients with harmful methods because of our ignorance. Therefore, intention may be good but the action may be bad (leading to bad consequences) and there is no reason why we should equate intention and action.

Third, after the concept of good will Kant introduces the concept of *duty* which means obligation to act in accordance with good will. He claims that any action is good not because it leads to good consequences and not because an actor has some internal kindness to help others, but because the actor understands that there is moral duty to act like this and acts for the sake of duty. Only an action *from* duty has "inner moral worth" but not an action *in conformity* with duty.

> For example, it certainly conforms with duty that a shopkeeper not over-charge an inexperienced customer, and where there is a good deal of trade a prudent merchant does not overcharge but keeps a fixed general price for everyone, so that a child can buy from him as well as everyone else. People are thus served honestly; but this is not nearly enough for us to believe that the merchant acted in this way from duty and basic principles of honesty; his advantage required it; it cannot be assumed here that he had, besides, an immediate inclination toward his customers, so as from love, as it were, to give no one preference over another in the matter of price. Thus the action was done neither from duty nor from immediate inclination but merely for purposes of self-interest. (*Groundwork*, p. 11)

This concept appears to be a serious departure from the scientific approach. First, it assumes that moral law has autonomous value but it is not proved. Moral laws may be good *because* they protect people's interests. So people follow any law to achieve this purpose. Does it make any sense to say that people are good *only when* they follow the moral law *for the sake of moral law*? Second, even if we agree that genuine moral behavior is to act for the sake of duty, what is the theoretical or practical value of this? This definitional nuance does not change the moral choice. A scientific moral theory can survive without this essentialism.

These methodological weaknesses are fully manifested in the derivation of Categorical Imperative. In Kant's terminology, every person may have some subjective principles of volition which are called *maxims* (e.g. a person has an individual rule to behave in a certain way). Besides this, there is a *duty* (moral law), an objective principle which any person with reason can discover a priori. Every person should understand that there is only one fundamental duty or moral law:

> I ought never to act except in such a way that I could also will that my maxim should become a universal law. (*Groundwork*, p. 15)

Kant uses as an example the problem of lying. A person should ask oneself if one wishes to live in a world where everyone tells lies. In Kantian logic the answer is "no" because in such a world there will be no promises at all because everyone will know that one's partner may lie.

> For in accordance with such a law there would properly be no promises at all, since it would be futile to avow my will with regard to my future actions to others who would not believe this avowal or, if they rashly did so, would pay me back in like coin; and thus my maxim, as soon as it were made a universal law, would have to destroy itself. (*Groundwork*, p. 15)

There are two weaknesses in this logic. First, "to destroy itself" is an incorrect conclusion. Such a world *can* exist and there will be contracts in this world (e.g. the economic theory of contracts teaches us that there are contractual remedies for enforcing contracts even in the world of complete cheaters). The real problem is that this world is *less efficient* because transactional costs of living in this world are higher. So, a rational actor will prefer the world *with* moral law which requires one to speak truth than the world *without* such a law. But here we come to the second problem of

Kantian logic. *How does the person decide which state of the world is better?* Why is the world without promises worse that the world with promises? This conclusion can be made only on the basis of rational choice. However, Kantian's framework does not have this concept. Maybe a concept of *good* can explain this choice? The answer is negative because there is no definition of good in the Kantian framework.

Therefore, Kantian moral theory has several weak points which make it incomplete or unproven. This is why it actually leads to many erroneous statements in further analysis. Let us consider the next example.

> Another finds himself urged by need to borrow money. He well knows that he will not be able to repay it but sees also that nothing will be lent him unless he promises firmly to repay it within a determinate time. He would like to make such a promise, but he still has enough conscience to ask himself: is it not forbidden and contrary to duty to help oneself out of need in such a way? Supposing that he still decided to do so, his maxim of action would go as follows: when I believe myself to be in need of money I shall borrow money and promise to repay it, even though I know that this will never happen. Now this principle of self-love or personal advantage is perhaps quite consistent with my whole future welfare, but the question now is whether it is right. I therefore turn the demand of self-love into a universal law and put the question as follows: how would it be if my maxim became a universal law? I then see at once that it could never hold as a universal law of nature and be consistent with itself, but must necessarily contradict itself. For, the universality of a law that everyone, when he believes himself to be in need, could promise whatever he pleases with the intention of not keeping it would make the promise and the end one might have in it itself impossible, since no one would believe what was promised him but would laugh at all such expressions as vain pretenses. (*Groundwork*, p. 32)

This is another example of incomplete logic. It seems that Kant wants to find a logical contradiction that may be derived by Pure Reason, but his explanation appears naïve. What does the expression "quite consistent with my whole future welfare" mean? If I fail to repay credit, all my future business transactions may be under question and my whole future welfare will be quite miserable. That is why in reality people may pay back all loans because of self-love and desire to keep their reputation for future transactions. In other words, an efficient loan market may exist pretty well without Kantian law but with Kantian law it will exist even better with lower transaction costs. It was well explained by Adam Smith in his *Theory of Moral Sentiments*.

Lack of explicit definitions of good and of rational action is the most serious methodological limitation of Kantian framework. However, implicit assumptions of rational choice and even utilitarian values may be found on the pages of *Groundwork*. For example, in the next fragment we can easily find the idea that one should maximize happiness of all members of society.

> concerning meritorious duty to others, the natural end that all human beings have is their own happiness. Now, humanity might indeed subsist if no one contributed to the happiness of others but yet did not intentionally withdraw anything from it; but there is still only a negative and not a positive agreement with humanity as an end in itself unless everyone also tries, as far as he can, to further the ends of others. For, the ends of a subject who is an end in itself must as far as possible be also my ends, if that representation is to have its full effect in me. (*Groundwork*, p. 39)

Still, Kant was able to make a giant step toward the scientific approach to ethics when he suggested the moral norms may be discovered and proved by any person autonomously from other people and every person should logically discover the same—universal—moral norms. This idea made Kant sure that only his framework provided a really true basis for morality.

> If we look back upon all previous efforts that have ever been made to discover the principle of morality, we need not wonder now why all of them had to fail. It was seen that the human being is bound to laws by his duty, but it never occurred to them that he is subject only to laws given by himself but still universal and that he is bound only to act in conformity with his own will, which, however, in accordance with nature's end is a will giving universal law. (*Groundwork*, p. 40)

The only problem is that Pure Reason alone cannot justify a non-tautological moral theory. That is why the frameworks of Hobbes or Mill had more elements of scientific ethics than the Kantian one.

HENRY SIDGWICK

The last person who made a contribution to development of a scientific approach in the nineteenth century was *Henry Sidgwick* (1838–1900)—a professor of moral philosophy in Cambridge University. Interestingly,

Sidgwick was also an economist. He was influenced by John Stuart Mill and significantly influenced A. Marshal who later called him "spiritual mother and father." In 1883 Sidgwick published a textbook *Principles of Political Economy* where he paid much attention to the methodology of economics as a science (study of production, distribution and exchange) and an art (government regulation). He did not distinguish positive from normative economics and his *Principles* have several chapters devoted to justice of distribution and moral evaluation of economic behavior (e.g. taking advantage over a partner using his ignorance about some facts). Obviously, his main interest was ethics.

In 1874 Sidgwick published *Methods of Ethics* which purpose was to explore "the different methods of obtaining reasoned convictions as to what ought to be done." In the beginning Sidgwick says that ethics should be built like other natural sciences, but prefer to call it "study" instead of "science" because its subject does not exist in the material world.

> ...the predominance in the minds of moralists of a desire to edify has impeded the real progress of ethical science: and that this would be bene-fited by an application to it of the same disinterested curiosity to which we chiefly owe the great discoveries of physics.
>
> The student of Ethics seeks to attain systematic and precise general knowledge of what ought to be, and in this sense his aims and methods may properly be termed scientific: but I have preferred to call Ethics a study rather than a science, because it is widely thought that a Science must neces-sarily have some department of actual existence for its subject-matter.

Sometimes it seems that Sidgwick suggests that all disagreement between various theories should be removed because there can be only one true theory of ethics.

> We cannot, of course, regard as valid reasonings that lead to conflicting conclusions; and I therefore assume as a fundamental postulate of Ethics, that so far as two methods conflict, one or other of them must be modified or rejected.

However, the main idea of his book was not to prove that one of these theories is better or genuinely true. He just wanted to examine several methods "from a neutral position, and as impartially as possible." By a "method of ethics" Sidgwick means "any rational procedure by which we determine what individual human beings *ought*—or what it is *right* for them—to do." Therefore, "methods" are used to derive "principles." Sidgwick takes three methods—egoism, intuitivism, and Utilitarianism—and examines the logic of argumentation in all of them. Eventually he demonstrates that actually these approaches are quite compatible and do not contradict each other. He did not build a unifying scientific framework of ethics and probably was satisfied that he successfully demonstrated that the three methods are compatible.

There is one methodological problem in his work. Sidgwick examines the methods of moral reasoning as they are used by ordinary people—he calls it "common sense morality" or a study of "moral consciousness of mankind." However, this is not a normative but *positive* ethics. It examines people who tend to argue about ethics and what historical traditions developed from various ideas. Even if we apply the best logic and evidence for critical study of these common-sense systems it does not lead to building of a normative theory.

For example, chapter 3 "Ethical Judgments" (Book I) offers a long discussion of what "X ought to be done" may mean to people. It looks like the meta-ethics debates of the 1930s (discussed in the next chapter) and may belong to lexicography, psychology, or sociology, but not to normative ethics. In a scientific approach to normative ethics we should not discuss ordinary language issues but define the theoretical concepts we need in the first pages and then found a theory on these clear and distinct concepts.

Sometimes it seems that common sense for Sidgwick was not "ordinary people thinking" but a kind of rational choice. But there was no concept of rational choice at that time (although Sidgwick does use the expression "rational choice" several times in the book but as an ordinary language expression, not a concept from future neoclassical economics). Probably, if Sidgwick were to write his treatise today, he would have said "rational choice morality" instead of "common sense morality" and his argumentation would be rendered somewhat differently.

In some aspects Sidgwick came very close to the scientific approach of ethics. For example, in the part about intuitivism, Sidgwick explores the so-called self-evidence principle of proof. After some consideration he suggests four conditions which make a proposition self-evident and which are very close to our criteria of scientific method:

- "The terms of the proposition must be clear and precise."
- "The self-evidence of the proposition must be ascertained by careful reflection."
- "The propositions accepted as self-evident must be mutually consistent."
- "Universal" or "general" consent has often been held to constitute by itself a sufficient evidence of the truth of the most important Beliefs; and is practically the only evidence upon which the greater part of mankind can rely."

Two approaches are very similar but instead of a "self-evident" concept (which actually was not well defined in Sidgwick's book) he used the concept of person's agreement with a proposition. Another difference is the absence of idea of collective choice in Sidgwick's work and the idea of veil of ignorance. (These concepts will appear only in the twentieth century.)

Sidgwick came very close to developing scientific ethics in some other aspects as well. For example, he suggested that there should be cooperation of normative and positive sciences. Good normative analysis should be always based on a good positive theory explaining the reality.

> On any theory, our view of what *ought* to be must be largely derived, in details, from our apprehension of what *is*

Another interesting idea was implicit distinction between the first best and second best moral choice (Sidgwick calls them Ideal and Positive law). Ideal moral norms may be unattainable in real societies with rigid institutions so we need to seek the second best choice and adapt to these institutions (a similar idea will be suggested as Integral Social Contract Theory in business ethics literature in 1980s).

> Suppose I am a slave-owner in a society in which slavery is established, and become convinced that private property in human beings should be abolished by law: it does not therefore follow that I shall regard it as my moral duty to set free my slaves at once. I may think immediate general abolition of slavery not only hopeless, but even inexpedient for the slaves themselves, who require a gradual education for freedom: so that it is better for the present to aim at legal changes that would cut off the worst evils of slavery, and meanwhile to set an example of humane and considerate treatment of bondsmen. (p. 17)

Interestingly, Sidgwick was one of the first moral philosophers who responded to Darwin's theory and evaluated its implications. In his paper "The Theory of Evolution in its Application to Practice" (1876) he claimed that "the theory of Evolution, thus widely understood, has little or no bearing upon ethics," meaning that normative conclusions do not depend on "moral faculty" developed during evolution.

> So long as the moral faculty was regarded as really a faculty of 'intuition' or rational apprehension of objective right and wrong, the history of these intuitions could seem of no more importance to the moralist as such than the history of our perception of space is to the geometer as such.

This is a very important principle assuming that emotional and intuitive argumentation cannot be used as a proof in the scientific approach to ethics.

CONCLUSION

We can summarize this brief survey of the historical development of ethics as follows:

- Ancient philosophers did not know the idea of science but still chose a rational approach to ethics which would later become a foundation for scientific ethics.
- Appearance of scientific method in the seventeenth century made several philosophers believe that ethics may also be built like a science.
- Almost all elements of scientific approach to ethics appeared in the writings of various scholars from the seventeenth to nineteenth centuries.
- The scholars who came the closest to scientific ethics were Hobbes and Mill.
- Kantian moral theory which is sometimes thought to be a superior philosophical construction has serious limitations from the scientific point of view.
- Virtue ethics, Utilitarianism and Deontology were often intertwined in the writings of many moral philosophers from the seventeenth to nineteenth centuries. The separation into three distinct approaches in the twentieth century would seem strange to them.

Notes

1. Bacon divided all sciences into Natural Philosophy and Human Philosophy. The latter was divided into Philosophy of Humanity which studies a man as such and Civil Philosophy which studies interaction of people in society. Philosophy of Humanity is divided into *study of body* and *study of soul*, and the study of soul was divided into two parts: *logic* which studies cognitive reasoning and *ethics* which studies will, the appetites, and affections. Ethics also consisted from two parts: "exemplar of platform of good" which should establish an ideal of good and "the regiment or culture of the mind" which should bring the person to the discovered ideal.

2. Descartes' *Method* was published in 1637, Hobbes' *Leviathan* in 1651. During his long stay in Paris, Hobbes enjoyed the intellectual company of skeptics (Maren Mersenne, Pierre Gassendi, and others), and therefore breathed the same intellectual atmosphere as Descartes (Herbert 2011, p. x). We know that Hobbes wrote a review on one of Descartes' books, and Descartes once said that Hobbes' "ability in morals was far greater than in metaphysics and physics." (Robertson 1886, p. 58). Leo Strauss suggested that Hobbes borrowed his understanding of passions from Descartes' *The Passions of the Soul* (1649) (Strauss 1936).

References

Asmis, Elizabeth. 1984. *Epicurus' Scientific Method*. Ithaca, NY: Cornell University Press.

Black, Max. 1964. The Gap Between "Is" and "Should". *The Philosophical Review* 73 (2): 165.

Box, Ian. 1996. Bacon's Moral Philosophy. In *The Cambridge Companion to Bacon*, ed. M. Peltonen, 260–282. New York: Cambridge University Press.

Caluori, Damian. 2007. The Scepticism of Francisco Sanchez. *Archiv für Geschichte der Philosophie* 89 (1): 30–46.

Descartes, René. 1985. *The Philosophical Writings of Descartes*. Vol. 1–2. Cambridge: Cambridge University Press.

Filmer, Robert. 1648. *The Necessity of the Absolute Power of All Kings*. London.

Finn, Stephen J. 2006. *Thomas Hobbes and the Politics of Natural Philosophy*. London: Bloomsbury Publishing.

Hare, Richard. 1952. *The Language of Morals*. Oxford: Clarendon Press.

Herbert, Gary B. 2011. *Thomas Hobbes: The Unity of Scientific and Moral Wisdom*. UBC Press.

Hobbes, Thomas. 1839. *The English Works of Thomas Hobbes of Malmesbury*. Edited by W. Molesworth, Vols. 1–11. London: J. Bohn.

Hume, David. 1739. *A Treatise of Human Nature*. London: Printed for John Noon.

Hutcheson, Francis. 1725. *An Inquiry into the Original of Our Ideas of Beauty and Virtue*. Printed by J. Darby in London.

Kant, Immanuel. 1998. *Groundwork of the Metaphysics of Morals*. Translated and edited by Mary Gregor, with an introduction by Christine M. Korsgaard. Cambridge: Cambridge University Press. (2006).

Locke, John. 1824. *The Works of John Locke in Nine Volumes*. 12th ed. London: Rivington.

Posner, Richard A. 1976. Blackstone and Bentham. *The Journal of Law and Economics* 19 (3): 569–606.

Price, Richard. 1758. *A Review of the Principal Questions and Difficulties in Morals: Particularly Those Relating to the Original of Our Ideas of Virtue, Its Nature, Foundation, Reference to the Deity, Obligation, Subject Matter, and Sanctions*. London: printed for A. Millar.

Raphael, David Daiches. 2007. *The Impartial Spectator: Adam Smith's Moral Philosophy*. Oxford: Oxford University Press.

Robertson, George Croom. 1886. *Hobbes*. Edinburgh: William Blackwood and Sons.

Smith, Adam. 1759. *The Theory of Moral Sentiments*. London: printed for A. Millar; and A. Kincaid and J. Bell, in Edinburgh.

Strauss, Leo. 1936. *The Political Philosophy of Thomas Hobbes: Its Basis and Its Genesis*. Translated by Elsa M. Sinclair. Oxford: Clarendon.

CHAPTER 5

Moore, Vienna Circle, and Meta-Ethics

Abstract In this chapter we will review the development of moral philoso-phy in the first half of the twentieth century when the discipline was strongly influenced by Moore with much skepticism about ethics and by logical positivism with its emphasis on the language. As a result moral philosophers immersed themselves in long debates for clarification of moral language and produced a vast literature called "meta-ethics" which is of rather unclear value for the further development of moral philosophy.

Keywords Moore • naturalistic fallacy • Vienna Circle • meta-ethics

GEORGE MOORE AND DENIAL OF ETHICS

In the early twentieth century the methodology of moral philosophy was impacted by one of the founders of the analytical tradition in philosophy, an English scholar *George Edward Moore* (1873–1958). In 1903 he pub-lished his famous *Principia Ethica* where he made a serious attack on any attempt to build an objective ethical theory. He tried to prove once more that it is impossible to derive "ought" from "is" and introduced the term *naturalistic fallacy* for those who make this mistake. Let us discuss this idea more carefully.

The first strong methodological claim of Moore is that it is impossible to define "good." Moore claims that "good" is a simple quality like "yel-low." Yellow is yellow and good is good, and no other definition is possible.

© The Author(s) 2018
M. Storchevoy, *A Scientific Approach to Ethics*,
https://doi.org/10.1007/978-3-319-69113-8_5

What follows from this thesis, by Moore, is that all propositions about good are synthetic and not analytic.

> If I am asked, "What is good?" my answer is that good is good, and that is the end of the matter. Or if I am asked "How is good to be defined?" my answer is that it cannot be defined, and that is all I have to say about it. But disappointing as these answers may appear, they are of the very last importance. To readers who are familiar with philosophic terminology, I can express their importance by saying that they amount to this: That propositions about the good are all of them synthetic and never analytic; and that is plainly no trivial matter. And the same thing may be expressed more popularly, by saying that, if I am right, then nobody can foist upon us such an axiom as that "Pleasure is the only good" or that "The good is the desired" on the pretence that this is "the very meaning of the word." (*Principia Ethica*, p. 6)
>
> My point is that good is a simple notion, just as yellow is a simple notion; that, just as you cannot, by any manner of means, explain to anyone who does not already know it, what yellow is, so you cannot explain what good is. (*Principia Ethica*, p. 7)

There is an obvious methodological confusion in this approach, and it is hard to explain how this confusion may occur because Moore seems to understand all general methodological premises which should prevent this mistake. First, "good" and "yellow" are words *in common language* which have meanings as to what ordinary people mean by them, and these meanings are studied by a lexicographer. Besides this they *may be defined* as any other word. For example, "yellow" may be defined as a "color which a normal human eye is experiencing when looking at the light with wavelength of 570–590 nanometers." "Good" may be defined as a "quality meaning that the phenomenon described by this quality are approved or desirable." These definitions are quite legitimate, but it is a subject of lexicography. The last fact is also acknowledged by Moore who declares that he does not want to deal with a lexicographical problem.

Second, in a scientific approach a scholar should define terms as it is necessary to build a productive discipline, e.g. "good" may be defined in a meaningful way in the beginning of ethical theory. Moore does not provide any logical proof that it is impossible. Actually, this problem of accurate and meaningful definition of "good" was successfully solved by many of Moore's predecessors (see Hobbes or Locke in the previous chapter).

We may define "good" as "what a person desires," but surprisingly, this approach was explicitly and without any reasons refused by Moore (see the citation above).

The next famous claim of Moore is about the so-called *naturalistic fallacy*. Moore says that it is wrong to derive "good" on the basis of some natural qualities like "large," "sweet," "pleasant," or "desirable." One can assign the quality of "good" to "sweet" but it is wrong to say that they are equivalent. Therefore, Moore makes a conclusion that if "good" is not a simple property, it should be: (1) a combination of properties or (2) a meaningless concept.

> In fact, if it is not the case that good denotes something simple and indefinable, only two alternatives are possible: either it is a complex, a given whole, about the correct analysis of which there may be disagreement; or else it means nothing at all, and there is no such subject as Ethics. In general, however, ethical philosophers have attempted to define good, without recognising what such an attempt must mean. They actually use arguments which involve one or both of the absurdities considered in 11. We are, therefore, justified in concluding that the attempt to define good is chiefly due to want of clearness as to the possible nature of definition. There are, in fact, only two serious alternatives to be considered, in order to establish the conclusion that good does denote a simple and indefinable notion. It might possibly denote a complex, as horse does; or it might have no meaning at all. Neither of these possibilities has, however, been clearly conceived and seriously maintained, as such, by those who presume to define good; and both may be dismissed by a simple appeal to facts. (*Principia Ethica*, p. 15)

However, this argument seems to be wrong from the very beginning. There is no proof that "only two alternatives are possible." What if we define "good" as "desired by a person"? It is not a property of the thing itself ("natural"), it is a property of personal choice. It is not a combination of the properties and it is meaningful. Why does Moore miss this variant of definition? It seems that Moore does understand the possibility of this approach but he rejects it because of the next argument.

The third famous claim made by Moore is known as the *Open Question Argument*. Moore writes that if we say that A is good because this is what we desire, it is possible to ask the next question: "Is it good that we desire A?" or in other words "Do we desire to desire A?" And if we answer this question in the confirmative, it is possible to ask the next question "Do we desire to desire to desire A?" In other words, regardless of our propositions about "good" it is always possible to ask if our proposition is good.

> The hypothesis that disagreement about the meaning of good is disagreement with regard to the correct analysis of a given whole, may be most plainly seen to be incorrect by consideration of the fact that, whatever definition be offered, it may be always asked, with significance, of the complex so defined, whether it is itself good. To take, for instance, one of the more plausible, because one of the more complicated, of such proposed definitions, it may easily be thought, at first sight, that to be good may mean to be that which we desire to desire. Thus if we apply this definition to a particular instance and say "When we think that A is good, we are thinking that A is one of the things which we desire to desire" our proposition may seem quite plausible. But, if we carry the investigation further, and ask ourselves "Is it good to desire to desire A"? It is apparent, on a little reflection, that this question is itself as intelligible, as the original question "Is A good?"— that we are, in fact, now asking for exactly the same information about the desire to desire A for which we formerly asked with regard to A itself. But it is also apparent that the meaning of this second question cannot be correctly analysed into "Is the desire to desire A one of the things which we desire to desire?": we have not before our minds anything so complicated as the question "Do we desire to desire to desire to desire A"? Moreover any one can easily convince himself by inspection that the predicate of this proposition— "good"—is positively different from the notion of "desiring to desire" which enters into its subject: "That we should desire to desire A is good" is *not* merely equivalent to "That A should be good is good". It may indeed be true that what we desire to desire is always also good; perhaps, even the converse may be true: but it is very doubtful whether this is the case, and the mere fact that we understand very well what is meant by doubting it, shews clearly that we have two different notions before our minds. (*Principia Ethica*, pp. 15–16)

This is a brilliant analytical move. However, it may lead moral philosophy nowhere. Fortunately, we have a solution. In our scientific variant of normative ethics such a question is meaningless. First, we defined "good" as "what a person desires under full information and controlling emotions" and by this *we methodologically moved into the domain of positive science* where our task is to reveal rational choice of an individual under certain conditions. Asking "is it good that we defined 'good' in that way" is simply beyond the scope of our theory because we study a positive task and do not evaluate it.

Second, we may interpret the Open Question Argument in another meaningful way if we imagine that the person asks herself *if she desires to be in this situation out of choice* (which is studied by our theory). In this case we implicitly assume that there are *some other alternatives* than being in this situation of choice, e.g. to be born in some other universe or not to be born at all. This is a wonderful question and a rational person will answer in a simple way: "Yes, I desire to be born in a better universe, so I do not want to be born in this one." In other words, the Open Question Argument may be reduced to another question "Is this the best possible universe?" and the answer for this question should be negative. It seems that everyone can imagine a better universe relating to one's preferences, but even if there might be disagreement on this issue, *what is the theoretical value of this discussion?* This discussion, regardless of its conclusions, does not undermine the scientific approach to ethics for people who are *already born* in our universe and cannot choose otherwise. These people will have to choose norms for this universe and our theory studies how they want to choose them. Open Question Argument is of no use here.

VIENNA CIRCLE AND LINGUISTIC TURN

In the first decades of the twentieth century there were serious advancements in the scientific approach to philosophy. Many philosophers, mathematicians, and other scholars from various countries were enthusiastic about reconsidering general scientific methodology and at the same time about rebuilding philosophy and science in a more accurate and systematic way to avoid two problems: (1) incompatible frameworks for various philosophical traditions and (2) to avoid all metaphysical elements which actually do not add new knowledge because they are meaningless, wrong, or unverifiable.

The leading role in this process was conducted by the *Vienna Circle*—a group of philosophers and scientists who met from time to time in the University of Vienna from 1907 to 1936. The first impact was done by *Ernst Mach* (1838–1916)—an Austrian physicist and philosopher who was the chair for "history and philosophy of the inductive sciences" in the University of Vienna from 1895 to 1901. He developed a new variant of empiricist methodology where the deductive theory was used not to model something that "exists as such" but to describe observed phenomena in the simplest and most economical way. For example, he suggested abandoning the concept of atoms which were unobservable at that time if it was possible to describe the reality in a simpler way. He suggested a veri-fication criterion of science ("where neither confirmation nor refutation is possible, science is not concerned"). The first discussions of Mach's philosophy of science in Vienna were started in 1907 in by a mathemati-cian Hans Hahn, an economist and historian Otto Neurath, and a physi-cist Philipp Frank. The participants of these discussions were numerous including famous British scholars like Bertrand Russell, Alfred Whitehead, Karl Popper, and others. After 1920 the Vienna Circle was inspired and coordinated by Moritz Schlick and in 1928 they even established the *Ernst Mach Society* to popularize scientific philosophy through public lectures, and published a manifesto *The Scientific Conception of the World*. In the 1930s the activity of this project was disintegrated step by step under political pressure of the new fascist regimes.

A methodological credo of Vienna Circle may be summarized as: (1) a unified science which includes philosophy as the most general knowledge, (2) no more metaphysical theorizing, and (3) the key to success is clear language, strict logic, and empirical verification. However, although many scholars from the Vienna Circle were very optimistic about building a new foundation for science and philosophy, *not one of them recognized moral philosophy as a good candidate for scientific status.*

In the 1910s an Austrian-British philosopher *Ludwig Wittgenstein* (1889–1951) wrote *Tractatus Logico-Philosophicus* (published in 1922) which became very popular among philosophers for its revolutionary attempt to construct an ideal language for philosophy on the basis of ordi-nary language. Wittgenstein tried to construct all philosophical knowl-edge from scratch using only accurately defined terms with accurate syntax. However, he denied this honor to ethics. The whole subject of ethics was placed by Wittgenstein in "the mystical, inexpressible region" (B. Russel, Introduction to *Tractatus Logico-Philosophicus*). Wittgenstein comes to ethics in the middle of his *Tractatus* in proposition 6.42 which reads "Hence also there can be no ethical propositions" because they express something which is beyond our observations. By Wittgenstein, an obvious proof of this thesis is a situation when one violates moral norms and nothing happens, which means that the word "ought" in this moral norm does not mean anything.

The first thought in setting up an ethical law of the form "thou shalt... " is: And what if I do not do it. But it is clear that ethics has nothing to do with punishment and reward in the ordinary sense. This question as to the consequences of an action must therefore be irrelevant. At least these consequences will not be events. For there must be something right in that formulation of the question. There must be some sort of ethical reward and ethical punishment, but this must lie in the action itself. (And this is clear also that the reward must be something acceptable, and the punishment something unacceptable.)

Once more the main cause of failure to develop an ethical theory starts with accurate definitions. Why did Wittgenstein decide that "ought" should necessarily be connected with rewards and punishment which is conduced automatically by nature if this is a socially constructed concept and rewards and punishments are designed by the society? It seems that Wittgenstein was very far from the domain of ethical thought.

An Austrian philosopher *Otto Neurath* (1882–1945) in the paper *"Sociology in the Framework of Physicalism"* (1932) discusses the possibility of building a scientific variant of ethics. Neurath assumes that there should be no division for natural and mental or social sciences because all phenomena must be described by a united science with united language. All psychological phenomena like emotions or perceptions are also physical by nature so they can be described in a unified language. Then Neurath asks how should we understand the role of ethics in this context? Traditionally, ethics was a study of divine command developed by Catholic thought. Probably God and divine punishment and reward may be also interpreted in a physicalist nature, but it is impossible to verify them up to the moment. Therefore, without God normative ethics loses its foundation and cannot be a science. However, Neurath suggests that we can study the behavior of people who make their choices seeking happiness and this is the only scientific discipline which should take the place of the old moral philosophy.

But how should we demarcate a discipline as 'ethics' if God is eliminated? Can we make a meaningful transition to a 'command' in itself to the 'categorical imperative'? We could just as well introduce a 'neighbour-in-himself without a neighbour', a 'son-in-himself who has never had father or mother'. How should certain commands or ways of behaviour be defined to make a 'new ethics within the framework of physicalism' possible? It seems to be impossible. Men can take common resolutions to behave somehow, and the consequences of such action can be investigated. But which ways of behaviour, which directions, should be distinguished as 'ethical' in order to establish correlations?

The continued use of an old name is based on the opinion that we can find something permanent that is common to the old theological or metaphysical and the new empiricist discipline. If all metaphysical elements are removed from ethics, as well as all theological physicalisms, then what remains is only either statements about certain ways of behaviour of men, or their commands to other men.

However, we could also think of a discipline, which, within the framework of unified science investigates in a perfectly behaviourist manner which responses are stimulated by a certain order of life, whether men become happier or less happy by certain orders of life. A perfectly empirical 'felicitology' could be devised on a behaviourist basis; it could take the place of traditional ethics. (*Sociology in the Framework of Physicalism*, p. 79)

A similar view was expounded by a German-American philosopher *Rudolf Carnap* (1891–1970) in the book *Philosophy and Logical Syntax* (1935). Carnap admitted that there might be a scientific descriptive ethics or psychological ethics which studies real people's feelings and choices about various facts, but it is impossible to build a scientific normative ethics because its statement is not verifiable. Normative ethics belongs to metaphysics which is beyond the scientific domain.

The word "Ethics" is used in two different senses. Sometimes a certain empirical investigation is called "Ethics," viz. psychological and sociological investigations about the actions of human beings, especially regarding the origin of these actions from feelings and volitions and their effects upon other people. Ethics in this sense is an empirical, scientific investigation; it belongs to empirical science rather than to philosophy. Fundamentally different from this is ethics in the second sense, as the philosophy of moral values or moral norms, which one can designate normative ethics. This is not an investigation of facts, but a pretended investigation of what is good and what is evil, what it is right to do and what it is wrong to do. Thus the purpose of this philosophical, or normative, ethics is to state norms for human action or judgment about moral values.

It is easy to see that it is merely a difference of formulation, whether we state a norm or a value judgment. A norm or rule has an imperative form, for instance: "Do not kill!" The corresponding value judgment would be: "Killing is evil." This difference of formulation has become practically very important, especially for the development of philosophical thinking. The rule "Do not kill" has grammatically the imperative form and will therefore not be regarded as an assertion. But the value statement, "Killing is evil," although, like the rule, it is merely an expression of a certain wish, has the grammatical form of an assertive proposition. Most philosophers have been deceived by this form into thinking that a value statement is really an assertive proposition, and must be either true or false. Therefore they give reasons for their own value statements and try to disprove those of their opponents. But actually a value statement is nothing else than a command in a misleading grammatical form. It may have effects upon the actions of men, and these effects may either be in accordance with our wishes or not; but it is neither true nor false. It does not assert anything and can neither be proved nor disproved.

This is revealed as soon as we apply to such statements our method of logical analysis. From the statement "Killing is evil" we cannot deduce any proposition about future experiences. Thus this statement is not verifiable and has no theoretical sense, and the same thing is true of all other value statements.

This argument is correct with only one amendment: the two sentences "Killing is evil" and "Do not kill" pronounced by a person X may be reduced to a positive verifiable proposition "X does not want killing to exist" which may be used to start building the scientific normative ethics.

A British philosopher *Bertrand Russell* (1872–1970) devoted his first significant works to the philosophical foundations of mathematics, writing *The Principles of Mathematics* (1903) and, with A. N. Whitehead, *Principia Mathematica* (1910). Russel tried to define a clear and systematic analysis of mathematical knowledge which he claimed was nothing more than formal logic.

Later Russell participated in the Vienna Circle discussions and spent much efforts to promote Wittgenstein's *Tractatus*.

In 1924 he published a small paper *Styles in Ethics* which was devoted mostly to sexual ethics but at the same time expressed his attitude about possibility of scientific approach to ethics.

Perhaps there is not, strictly speaking, any such thing as 'scientific' ethics. It is not the province of science to decide on the ends of life. Science can show that an ethic is unscientific, in the sense that it does not minister to any desired end. Science also can show how to bring the interest of the individual into harmony with that of society. We make laws against theft, in order that theft may become contrary to self-interest. We might, on the same ground, make laws to diminish the number of imbecile children born into the world. There is no evidence that existing marriage laws, particularly where they are very strict, serve any social purpose; in this sense we may say that they are unscientific. But to proclaim the ends of life, and make men conscious of their value, is not the business of science; it is the business of the mystic, the artist and the poet.

The same position was held by Russell during all his career. In his famous *History of Western Philosophy* he again asserts that ethics cannot be part of science because scientific method is not applicable to the former. Ethics is more like religion where everyone can have their own beliefs.

There remains, however, a vast field, traditionally included in philosophy, where scientific methods are inadequate. This field includes ultimate questions of value; science alone, for example, cannot prove that it is bad to enjoy the infliction of cruelty. Whatever can be known, can be known by means of science; but things which are legitimately matters of feeling lie outside its province. (*A History of Western Philosophy*)

As we see from this short overview, the main philosophers of logical positivism explicitly denied the possibility of developing normative ethics as a science, mostly because they did not consider verification of its propositions. The key problem was with basic definitions of normative ethics which actually could be modified to make its propositions verifiable but this possibility was missed by the scholars.

META-ETHICAL DEBATES

Moore's criticism had a serious impact on further development of methodology of ethics. As we said in the previous section there was much skepticism in the first half of the twentieth century on this issue. Since the 1930s there were a lot of discussions of the terminology and moral language which led to the formation of *meta-ethics*—a special branch of moral philosophy studying the nature of ethical judgments. This discipline was focused on three interrelated questions (Garner and Rosen 1967, p. 215): (1) what is the meaning of moral terms or judgments, (2) what is the nature of moral judgments, and (3) how moral judgments may be supported or defended. The answer for one question in many cases predetermines the answer for other questions.

Meta-ethical discussions have continued up to today and produced a vast literature but its theoretic value remains quite unclear. These discussions have not led to resolution of terminological and methodological disagreement. Many core concepts in that literature are still defined by various authors in a diverse way which makes a precise classification of these concepts and approaches very difficult. And this is not good, because if there is no agreement between scholars about definitions of basic terms, it is hard to expect scientific progress in such a field. Why did this happen? There were no ideas of scientific methods of verification of propositions in these debates. As a result, much more alternative concepts and frameworks survived than it would be possible in traditional sciences like physics or economics. Below we will try to provide a short review of general meta-ethical ideas and we will see that there is actually no comprehensive "theory" behind one label. This is a language to describe moral theories.

A historical survey of development of meta-ethics may require a separate book, so we will only describe the outcome of these debates—the classification of main concepts. All moral philosophy may be divided into two branches: *cognitivism* that assumes possibility of moral propositions (e.g. "murder is wrong") that may be true or false, and *non-cognitivism* that assumes that these propositions cannot be true or false.

Cognitivism supposes that moral statements are meaningful and may be true or false. It means that ethics may be a science, because we can develop a theory explaining how to evaluate whether a moral statement is right or wrong. Cognitivism may be classified further according to four different dimensions (various epistemic aspects): (1) objectivism vs. non-objectivism vs. subjectivism, (2) absolutism vs. relativism, (3) realism vs. anti-realism, and (4) naturalism vs. non-naturalism. As you will see below, the boundaries between these dichotomies are blurred and it is not easy to distinguish one from another.

Moral objectivism vs. moral non-objectivism vs. subjectivism. Moral objectivism assumes that moral propositions may be true because of some objective facts that exist independently of the human mind (e.g. mind-independent facts, Joyce 2015). The best example of this seems to be Plato who believed that there was objective knowledge about the Form of Good that can be theoretically known although it is very difficult and no one has solved it yet. *Moral non-objectivism* assumes that there is no moral truth which does not depend on human mind (moral truth is construed by mental activity). A good example of this position is Shakespeare's line in *Hamlet*, "there is nothing either good or bad, but thinking makes it so," or Thomas Hobbes (see the previous chapter). Non-objectivism is not a synonym for *subjectivism* although these terms may be used interchangeably in some texts. Usually, subjectivism means that a moral proposition is made by a person and reflects her own mental attitude (Joice 2015, p. 4) and this attitude may be wrong. Some authors believe that the concepts of subjectivism and objectivism are impossible to define in a universally accepted way (Rosen 1994).

Moral absolutism vs. moral relativism. Moral absolutism supposes that there is only one universal moral truth which does not depend on the culture of the society. A good example of this view is Immanuel Kant and his moral law. Another example is the Ideal Observer theory (Firth 1952), although compared to Kant this theory admits that the correct moral choice may depend on the circumstances (e.g. lying may be good in one situation and wrong in another). *Moral relativism* assumes that moral truth depends on the culture of the society, and "the standards of justification in the two societies may differ from one another and that there is no rational basis for resolving these differences" (Gowans 2015, p. 6; Harman 1975). A variety of moral relativism theories was developed inside the business ethics domain (stakeholder theory, ISCT theory, etc.).

Moral realism vs. moral anti-realism. Moral realism assumes that moral propositions may be true or false depending on some external facts. It may seem that moral objectivism belongs to moral realism. For example, Rist (2002) calls Plato a moral realist and develops a contemporary framework on this approach. Some authors do not distinguish moral realism and objectivism at all (Bunnin and Yu 2008, p. 448). However, it is not clear if we should include moral non-objectivism into moral realism, because it depends on our definition of "real." Can we say that the moral truth shaped by mental activity is "real"? Some authors answer this positively and include various forms of subjectivism into moral realism (e.g. Sayre-McCord 1996). Some authors prefer more sophisticated definitions: *minimal moral realism* which combines objectivism and non-objectivism, and *robust moral realism* which includes only the latter (e.g. Joyce 2015). However, the obscure distinction between moral realism and anti-realism (Joice 2015, p. 28) as well as general realism and anti-realism makes these concepts so uninformative that modern philosophers would not accept them without further explanation.

> ...if there ever was a consensus of understanding about 'realism', as a philosophical term of art, it has undoubtedly been fragmented by the pressures exerted by the various debates—so much so that a philosopher who asserts that she is a realist about theoretical science, for example, or ethics, has probably, for most philosophical audiences, accomplished little more than to clear her throat. (Wright 1988)

Moral naturalism vs. moral non-naturalism. Moral naturalism assumes that "good" may be linked to some objective characteristics. For example, if we assume "good" means "pleasure" (as Bentham did) we would be moral naturalists. *Moral non-naturalism* assumes that this link is logically wrong and it is necessary to prove that "pleasure" is "good" (Moore and his "naturalistic fallacy"). However, there are some moral realists who try to prove that moral facts may be treated as natural facts or at least are compatible with these facts. For example, a representative of the so-called Cornel realism, Boyd (1988) suggests a "homeostatic consequentialism" which "identifies 'goodness' with a cluster of properties, conducive to satisfaction of human needs, tending to occur together and with a tendency to promote each other" (Lenman 2015, p. 29). Others believe that it is possible to express moral claims in only naturalistic terms (Jackson 1998; Finlay 2014). There are neo-Aristotelian naturalists (Foot 2001; Hursthouse 1999) who suggest that "good" is equivalent to "helping for reproduction and survival."

Non-cognitivism holds that ethical statements cannot be true or false because they do not describe anything, but express something other than facts. Essentially, this means impossibility of moral science. There are several variants of non-cognitivism. *Emotivism* assumes that moral propositions are generated by feelings and express only feelings, so they cannot be true or false. One on the earliest proponents of this view was David Hume who believed that ethics is just a subjective experience which can never be a science. Later, emotivism was supported in the twentieth century by several representatives of *logical positivism* who believed in verification principle of scientific knowledge but they viewed ethical statements as based on emotions (Malinowski et al. 1923; Ayer 1936; Stevenson 1937). Another branch of non-cognitivism is *universal prescriptivism* which states that ethical sentences do not describe but prescribe (Hare 1952).

Finally, there is the *moral error theory* (Mackie 1977) or *moral nihilism* (Harman 1977, p. 11) that occupies a middle position somewhere between cognitivism and non-cognitivism. It admits that moral propositions relate to facts and may be true or false (cognitivism), but all attempts of researchers will lead to false results. This is similar to atheist opinion about religion which assumes that all propositions about God are meaningful but they are all false. In other words, moral truth is unattainable. Why? There is disagreement between people about moral truth and it is impossible reconcile. Mackie assumes that moral truth should be supported by everyone but any particular moral norm will be rejected by someone because that one does not have internal desire to comply with it. So, universal moral truth does not exist. This approach implicitly allows for the existence of moral science, but believes that its main theorem is impossible to prove.

Many of these terminological distinctions of meta-ethics are orthogonal to each other, e.g. an objectivist may be naturalist or non-naturalist, absolutist or relativist, etc. There are no separate and distinctive theories beyond these labels. It is only a *language* of describing moral theories and it is not the best language, because there is no clear distinction between many of these terms (e.g. objectivism and realism) and there is no universal definition of many terms (e.g. what is "objective"). A detailed accurate terminology is a good thing, but, as some scholars admit, the obsession with terminological and linguistic debates eventually brought a sophisticated landscape and even wider disagreement.

> The moral philosophy of the first half of the twentieth century, at least in the English-speaking part of the world, has been largely devoted to problems concerning the analysis of ethical statements, and to correlative problems of an ontological or epistemological nature. This concentration of effort by many acute analytical minds has not produced any general agreement with respect to the solution of these problems; it seems likely, on the contrary, that the wealth of proposed solutions, each making some claim to plausibility, has resulted in greater disagreement than ever before, and in some cases disagreement about issues so fundamental that certain schools of thought now find it unrewarding, if not impossible, to communicate with one another. (Firth 1952, p. 317)

Why did this happen? I suggest that there was no desire to be scientific and use a scientific method to sort out all "unproductive" frameworks. There is no word "scientific" in the meta-ethical language, and you will almost never be part of a discussion of scientific method in this literature.

In the 1980s the toolbox of meta-ethics was supplied with one more term—"thick concept." It was suggested by *Bernard Williams* in his book, *Ethics and the Limits of Philosophy* (1985) to classify concepts that express a descriptive as well as evaluative meaning. Almost all names of virtues like *courageous* and *generous* have descriptive and evaluative meaning. Many names of actions like *murder* and *betray* also have them. Scholars thought that thick concepts may provide additional insight into meta-ethical disputes about ethical truth or fact-value distinction. Some suggested that thick concepts may enhance normative ethics. However, the idea of thick concepts is based on the same false assumption as the meta-ethical perspective—that normative ethics which is a science constructed by scholars should depend on or be compatible with words and meanings of real people.

REFERENCES

Ayer, A.J. 1936. *Language, Truth and Logic*. Courier Corporation.

Boyd, Richard. 1988. How to Be a Moral Realist. In *Essays on Moral Realism*, ed. G. Sayre-McCord, 181–228. Ithaca, NY: Cornell University Press.

Bunnin, Nicholas, and Yu Jiyuan. 2008. *The Blackwell Dictionary of Western Philosophy*. John Wiley & Sons.

Finlay, Stephen. 2014. *Confusion of Tongues: A Theory of Normative Language*. Oxford: Oxford University Press.

Firth, Roderick. 1952. Ethical Absolutism and the Ideal Observer. *Philosophy and Phenomenological Research* 12 (3): 317–345.

Foot, Philippa. 2001. *Natural Goodness*. Oxford: Clarendon Press.

Garner, Richard T., and Bernard Rosen. 1967. *Moral Philosophy: A Systematic Introduction to Normative Ethics and Meta-ethics*, 215. New York: Macmillan.

Gowans, Chris. 2015. Moral Relativism. In *The Stanford Encyclopedia of Philosophy*, ed. Edward N. Zalta (Fall 2015 Edition). https://plato.stanford.edu/archives/fall2015/entries/moral-relativism/

Hare, Richard Mervyn. 1952. *The Language of Morals*. Oxford: Clarendon Press.

Harman, Gilbert. 1975. Moral Relativism Defended. *The Philosophical Review* 84 (1): 3–22.

Harman, Gilbert. 1977. *The Nature of Morality: An Introduction to Ethics*. New York: Oxford University Press.

Hursthouse, Rosalind. 1999. *On Virtue Ethics*. Oxford: Clarendon Press.

Jackson, Frank. 1998. *From Metaphysics to Ethics: A Defence of Conceptual Analysis*. Oxford: Oxford University Press.

Joyce, Richard. 2015. Moral Anti-Realism. In *The Stanford Encyclopedia of Philosophyi*, ed. Edward N. Zalta (Fall 2015 Edition). https://plato.stanford.edu/archives/fall2015/entries/moral-anti-realism/

Mackie, John Leslie. 1977. *Ethics: Inventing Right and Wrong*. Harmondsworth: Penguin.

Malinowski, Bronislaw, F.G. Crookshank, Charles Kay Ogden, and Ivor Armstrong Richards. 1923. *The Meaning of Meaning: A Study of the Influence of Language Upon Thought and of the Science of Symbolism*. Kegan Paul, Trench, Trubner & Co.

Neurath, O. 1932. *Sociology in the Framework of Physicalism//Philosophical Papers 1913–1946*; with a Bibliography of Neurath in English. Vol. 16. Springer Science & Business Media, 2012.

Rist, John M. 2002. *Real Ethics: Reconsidering the Foundations of Morality.* Cambridge University Press.

Rosen, Gideon. 1994. Objectivity and Modern Idealism: What Is the Question? *Philosophy in Mind,* 277–319.

Sayre-McCord, Geoffrey. 1996. Coherentist Epistemology and Moral Theory. In *Moral Knowledge: New Readings,* ed. Walter Sinnott-Armstrong and Mark Timmons, 137–189. New York: Oxford University Press.

Stevenson, Charles Leslie. 1937. The Emotive Meaning of Ethical Terms. *Mind* 46 (181): 14–31.

Wright, Crispin. 1988. Realism, Antirealism, Irrealism, Quasi-Realism. Gareth Evans Memorial Lecture, Delivered in Oxford on June 2, 1987. *Midwest Studies in Philosophy* 12 (1): 25–49.

CHAPTER 6

Contractarianism and Rational Choice

Abstract In this chapter we will survey the rational choice approaches for normative ethics developed in the second part of the twentieth century. Some of these approaches belong to contractarian ethics but our main focus will be not on a social contract but on rational choice. We will survey and evaluate the contributions of several prominent thinkers (Rawls, Nozick, Sen, Harsanyi, and Scanlon) from the lens of the scientific approach to ethics to demonstrate that its principles have a crucial importance to the progress on normative ethics.

Keywords contractarian ethics • rational choice • veil of ignorance • Rawls • Nozick • Gauthier • Scanlon

As you saw in the last two chapters, in the 1880s Henry Sidgwick proposed many elements of scientific approach to ethics in his critical analysis of alternative moral theories but he did not build a new theory which could replace them. Although Sidgwick was an influential figure, his belief in a scientific approach to ethics did not have much impact. A much stronger influence was Moore's denial of ethics and analytical philosophy. The methodology of normative ethics made a "linguistic turn" and transformed into meta-ethical debates which produced a vast literature of abstract concepts and frameworks—diverse, incompatible, and useless. Meanwhile the real progress of the scientific approach to ethics happened in applied areas—in political philosophy and public choice theory.

© The Author(s) 2018
M. Storchevoy, *A Scientific Approach to Ethics*,
https://doi.org/10.1007/978-3-319-69113-8_6

JOHN RAWLS

A significant development of the methodology of ethics was made by an American political and moral philosopher *John Rawls* (1921–2002) who focused on the problem of fairness in the process of moral norms choice. In his early paper *Justice as Fairness* (1958) Rawls suggested that the classical form of Utilitarianism may lead to unfair results. For example, classical Utilitarianism may formally justify slavery because the benefits to slaveholders may overshadow harm to slaves. However, this seems to be a sort of moral fallacy or "disorder in the conception of the ranking of moral principles." The highest principle of justice which should be put above of general happiness maximization is personal free choice. Therefore, all inequalities are morally permissible only if "the representative man in *every* office would find the inequality to his advantage."

> It should be noted that … an inequality is allowed only if there is reason to believe that the practice with the inequality, or resulting in it, will work for the advantage of every party engaging in it. Here it is important to stress that every party must gain from the inequality. (*Justice as Fairness*, p. 167)

Interestingly, in the paper *The Sense of Justice* (1963) Rawls paid tribute to intuitivism and tried to find a defense of justice in intuitive feelings about just and unjust actions which all people have. He claimed that a person must have a sense of justice to be allowed to participate in the initial norms choice process. *Sense of justice*, in this framework, plays the same key role as *good will* in Kantian theory.

> The capacity for a sense of justice is, then, necessary and sufficient for the duty of justice to be owed to a person—that is, for a person to be regarded as holding an initial position of equal liberty. This means that one's conduct in relation to him must be regulated by the principles of justice or, more generally, by the principles which rational and self-interested persons could acknowledge before one another in such a position. (*The Sense of Justice*, p. 304)

Later in his book *Theory of Justice* (1971) Rawls suggested a new interpretation of moral norms, based on rational choice. He described a fair procedure for derivation of universal moral norms which significantly expanded both the social contract frameworks of Hobbes and Locke and the Pure Reason framework of Kant. He assumed that moral norms for the society are chosen collectively and "the most reasonable principles of justice are those everyone would accept and agree to from a fair position."

> Just as each person must decide by rational reflection what constitutes his good, that is, the system of ends which it is rational for him to pursue, so a group of persons must decide once and for all what is to count among them as just and unjust. The choice which rational men would make in this hypothetical situation of equal liberty, assuming for the present that this choice problem has a solution, determines the principles of justice. (*Theory of Justice*, p. 10)

Essentially Rawls took the social contract theory and replaced the *state of nature* with *original position* which had an additional procedural constraint. In this original position all people are equal, rational, and free and have to choose the norms for the society where they will live. But in the original position they do not know anything about their physical characteristics and their place in the real society which does not exist yet. Each of them could become a man or a woman, black or white, healthy or ill, and so on with equal probability. The imaginary curtain that separates the original position from the real world is called *veil of ignorance*.[1] What norms will be chosen by people in that original position? Rawls claims that it would be two fundamental norms:

- Every person should have maximum personal freedom compatible with similar freedom of other people.
- The social system should maximize the material well-being of the most vulnerable (least-advantageous) people.

The first norm defends all minorities from potential abuse by majority. Heavy smoker, sybarite, homosexual, shamanist, etc.—everyone should have the right to a lifestyle one prefers. Majority cannot impose any restrictions on personal behavior if the behavior really does not threaten the well-being of other people (e.g. the rights of a maniac killer will not be defended in this society).

The second rule corrects unfair rewards caused by different initial resource endowments. In any type of economic system some people may get larger compensation because of advantages they have while starting out (better health, better capabilities, better financial position, better connections, etc.), so the difference in earnings will be caused not only by different efforts but also by different starting positions. Therefore, people in least-advantageous positions (unhealthy, disabled, orphans, kids from very poor families, etc.) will suffer from a very low compensation or no compensation at all. However, this is not their fault and they cannot change it. So in the original position people will vote for maximum social protection for these positions, because they rationally may expect that they may find themselves in these positions in the future.

Essentially it was a rational choice theory. People will vote for this norm because they do not know in which position they will find themselves in the real world and want to maximize their welfare and avoid potential suffering. Rawls assumed that this approach may be generalized to the whole ethics although he was skeptical that it was possible to include it into the theory of animals and nature.

However, Rawls was a bit skeptical that he may succeed in persuading others that this theory is correct.

> The problem of the choice of principles, however, is extremely difficult. I do not expect the answer I shall suggest to be convincing to everyone. (*Theory of Justice*, p. 14)

Rawls distinguished two concepts—*justification* (persuading a particular opponent) and *proof* (demonstration of logical connection between assumptions and conclusions).

> Justification is argument addressed to those who disagree with us, or to ourselves when we are of two minds. It presumes a clash of views between persons or within one person, and seeks to convince others, or ourselves, of the reasonableness of the principles upon which our claims and judgments are founded. Being designed to reconcile by reason, justification proceeds from what all parties to the discussion hold in common. Ideally, to justify a conception of justice to someone is to give him a proof of its principles from premises we both accept, these principles in turn having consequences that match our considered judgments. Thus mere proof is not justification. A proof simply displays logical relations between propositions. But proofs become justification once the starting points are mutually recognized, or the conclusions so comprehensive and compelling as to persuade us of the soundness of the conception expressed by their premises. (p. 508)

He did not hope to persuade everyone but just wanted to prove his theory on its own ground. However, even this proof was a bit strange from the traditional science point of view. Rawls tried to prove the original position framework as "the most philosophically favored interpretation" of the initial norms choice. However, what does "philosophically favored" mean?

> But how are we to decide what is the most favored interpretation? I assume, for one thing, that there is a broad measure of agreement that principles of justice should be chosen under certain conditions. To justify a particular description of the initial situation one shows that it incorporates these commonly shared presumptions. One argues from widely accepted but weak premises to more specific conclusions. Each of the presumptions should by itself be natural and plausible; some of them may seem innocuous or even trivial. The aim of the contract approach is to establish that taken together they impose significant bounds on acceptable principles of justice. The ideal outcome would be that these conditions determine a unique set of principles; but I shall be satisfied if they suffice to rank the main traditional conceptions of social justice.
>
> One should not be misled, then, by the somewhat unusual conditions which characterize the original position. The idea here is simply to make vivid to ourselves the restrictions that it seems reasonable to impose on arguments for principles of justice, and therefore on these principles themselves. Thus it seems reasonable and generally acceptable that no one should be advantaged or disadvantaged by natural fortune or social circumstances in the choice of principles. It also seems widely agreed that it should be impossible to tailor principles to the circumstances of one's own case. We should insure further that particular inclinations and aspirations, and persons' conceptions of their good do not affect the principles adopted. (*Theory of Justice*, pp. 16–17)

As we see, Rawls tries to find proof of his theory in two ways: (1) demonstrating that it is a most reasonable approach or rational choice and (2) assuming that its initial principles or conclusions will be very close to "commonly shared presumptions." However, he explicitly stated that he does not hope to achieve some absolute degree of persuasiveness.

> In arriving at the favored interpretation of the initial situation there is no point at which an appeal is made to self-evidence in the traditional sense either of general conceptions or particular convictions. I do not claim for the principles of justice proposed that they are necessary truths or derivable

from such truths. A conception of justice cannot be deduced from self-evident premises or conditions on principles; instead, its justification is a matter of the mutual support of many considerations, of everything fitting together into one coherent view. (*Theory of Justice*, p. 19)

Although Rawls made a significant contribution to the development of a scientific approach to ethics, he did not try to build a more formal proof of his theses. He tried to be persuasive and described his ideas as something natural or intuitively obvious. He hoped to develop a theory of true justice and even made a comparison of *justice* in social systems with *truth* in a system of thought. The task of building a fundamental "justification for everyone" remained unsolved. Unsurprisingly, his theory met with strong criticism from some philosophers who had other intuitions on that topic.

ROBERT NOZICK

The Rawlsian idea of fairness was criticized by an American philosopher *Robert Nozick* (1938–2002). In 1971 Nozick was lecturing on capitalism and socialism in Harvard University (with Michael Walzer), and on the basis of his lectures Nozick prepared a book *Anarchy, State, and Utopia* (1974). The book was well written and attracted the attention of philosophers due to its interesting arguments and polemics with Rawlsian concepts of justice. In this book Nozick developed many novel ideas like utility monster or experience machine which were very helpful in the discussion of moral dilemmas in various theories. Unfortunately, after this book Nozick did not write again on political or moral philosophy, becoming preoccupied with other philosophical problems.

What was his point of criticism of Rawlsian concept of justice? Nozick starts his book with the assumption that all people have rights and no one, including the state, can violate these rights.

Individuals have rights and there are things no person or group may do to them (without violating their rights). So strong and far-reaching are these rights that they raise the question of what, if anything, the state and its officials may do. How much room do individual rights leave for the state?

The rest of Nozick's argument is based on this assumption including the rejection of the principle that the state should maximize the well-being of the most vulnerable people. This looks like a serious methodological mistake. There are no natural moral rights, all rights are constructed by people's decisions, and their construction should be based on some moral theory. However, Nozick does not use any moral theory for justifying these rights. This looks like a mistake. It is impossible to build a political philosophy trying to answer the question "Do we really need the state?" independently of moral philosophy. First we need to answer fundamental questions like "Do we need universal moral norms" and "What should be these rights?" and only after this we should raise the question of political philosophy: "Which political system is the best to achieve these purposes?"

Nozick explicitly states that his focus is beyond moral philosophy and he will focus only on political philosophy and explanatory political theory (= positive political science).

> The completely accurate statement of the moral background including the precise statement of the moral theory and its underlying basis, would require a full-scale representation and is a task for another time. (p. 9)

Then he built a wonderful "explanatory" analysis of how people will protect themselves in the Lockean state of nature. They will create protective associations and one of these associations will eventually become dominant, i.e. a state will emerge. Then he introduces the concepts of *minimal state* (night-watchmen) and *ultraminimal state* (one gets protection of rights only after paying a fee) and discusses their comparative attractiveness. Here he comes to moral issues. Minimal state allows some violation of rights for a fuller protection of rights, and this is an element of redistribution. Is it good? Nozick provides a long and interesting discussion of how this question should be analyzed, including the choice between taking rights protection as a condition or a restraint and introducing the concept of "utilitarianism of rights" (maximization of weighted rights protection) and an adjusted variant of Categorical Imperative ("act as to minimize the use of humanity simply as a means"). Then he proceeds with an interesting discussion of permissibility of victims, including an innocent victim and innocent shield. He ends this discussion with a note that he wanted only to "tiptoe around them" and they require more systematic analysis. However, these questions may be correctly analyzed and resolved with the help of veil of ignorance.

In the Chap. 7 Nozick comes to analysis of Rawlsian theory and it seems that he completely loses his temperance trying to reject the difference principle. He provides hundreds of arguments which are smart and inventive but yet fails to reject the idea of veil of ignorance. His arguments do not look ultimately persuasive even if there is an interesting idea behind each of them. This is one example of an inventive argument.

> One indication of the stringency of Rawls' difference principle, which we attend co in the second part of chis chapter, is its inappropriateness as a governing principle even within a family of individuals who love one another. Should a family devote its resources to maximizing the position of its least well off and least talented child, holding back the other children or using resources for their education and development only if they will follow a policy through their lifetimes of maximizing the position of their lease fortunate sibling? Surely not. (p. 167)

This situation offers insufficient information to make a definite moral judgment, but Nozick still comes to a conclusion. A similar situation repeats itself many times with his other arguments. It seems that Nozick did not use a *definite method of proof* which should serve as a scientific method to reject wrong hypothesis. He tries to prove which principles are more *reasonable* but there was *no definition* of reasonability in the book. Nozick understands this methodological problem but it seems that he does not see any alternative.

> Since the sentences which precede it are neutral between his proposal and any other proposal, the conclusion that the difference principle presents a fair basis for cooperation cannot follow from what precedes it in this passage. Rawls is merely repeating that it seems reasonable; hardly a convincing reply co anyone to whom it doesn't seem reasonable. (p. 196)

This is not a scientific approach and it does not guarantee agreement between scholars ("it seems to Rawls reasonable and it does not seem to me"), and this is the first reason of Nozick's failure to reject Rawlsian theory. The second reason seems to be that Nozick was too focused on particular wording of the difference principle but the main contribution of Rawls was the method of derivation of moral norms—the idea of veil of ignorance. Did Nozick agree with this method? It seems so because his other ideas sound quite consonant. For example, his framework for utopia is essentially the first principle of Rawlsian justice (maximum personal freedom).

AMARTYA SEN

An American economist *Amartya Sen* (born 1933) with a strong interest in philosophy made several significant contributions to welfare economics, social choice, and poverty studies for which he was awarded the Nobel Prize in 1998.

One of these contributions was aimed at enhancing the Rawlsian approach to justice as fairness. In 1979 Sen delivered a lecture "Equality of What?" in Stanford University which was the first explanation of his approach to moral theory. Sen admitted a strong influence of Rawls but emphasized that he wanted to add some important aspects which are absent in Rawlsian theory. Interestingly, in the beginning of this lecture Sen raised the question of proof in ethical methodology. He refers to our "intuition" as a final judge in moral questions and introduces two methods: case-implication critique and prior-principle critique.

> When it is claimed that a certain moral principle has shortcomings, what can be the basis of such an allegation? There seem to be at least two different ways of grounding such a criticism, aside from just checking its direct appeal to moral intuition. One is to check the implications of the principle by taking up particular cases in which the results of employing that principle can be seen in a rather stark way, and then to examine these implications against our intuition. I shall call such a critique a *case-implication critique*. The other is to move not from the general to the particular, but from the general to the more general. One can examine the consistency of the principle with another principle that is acknowledged to be more fundamental. Such prior principles are usually formulated at a rather abstract level, and frequently take the form of congruence with some very general procedures. For example, what could be reasonably assumed to have been chosen under the as if ignorance of the Rawlsian "original position," a hypothetical primordial state in which people decide on what rules to adopt without knowing who they are going to be—as if they could end up being any one of the persons in the community. ...I shall call a critique based on such an approach a *prior-principle critique*. Both approaches can be used in assessing the moral claims of each type of equality, and will indeed be used here.

However, the rest of his analysis in this paper is very difficult to read because it seems that he does not use any method of proving his statements, and handles the criticized approaches rather carelessly. He criticizes "utilitarianism" although there was no well-defined version of Utilitarianism in the 1970s but many different understandings developed during the history of moral philosophy. His "utilitarian equality" and "total utility equality" just do not exist in well-developed theories.

The main idea of this paper is that a Rawlsian approach or "difference principle" fails when we introduce *various capabilities* of people. Sen's famous example is of cripples who cannot derive the same utility from the same primary goods as normal people. So a just society should compensate cripples for their inability to move, e.g. by providing them additional resources to increase their mobility. Essentially, this is quite a natural outcome for the Rawlsian method but the problem of different capabilities was discussed in his 1971 book, so Sen's discussion of capabilities was a correct and useful clarification of that aspect of Rawlsian approach. In the second edition of *Theory of Justice* in 1990, Rawls responded and changed the definition of primary goods to "what persons need in their status as free and equal citizens, and as normal and fully cooperating members of society over a complete life" which embraced the idea of equalizing capabilities.

This concept was named "capability approach" although it was not a new approach but just an adjustment in the basic Rawlsian choice of moral norms. It means that a person should assume the possibility of being born a cripple and wisely assume moral norms that help to compensate physical limitations.

In 2009 Sen published *The Idea of Justice* with a deeper analysis of moral theory. Although its table of content looks quite promising (many interesting questions about contractual approach and objectivity) the real analysis creates a feeling of general weakness of moral philosophy. The book offers his reflections on many aspects of moral philosophy but the author does not believe that moral theory may be constructed in a rigorous way and so his own analysis looks like a spontaneous essay on a given topic. Interestingly, this book also starts with an important claim about methodology of moral theory assuming that a moral truth may be proven in many different ways and although people may disagree about one particular way they agree that all the circumstances justify this moral truth.

> What is important to note here, as central to the idea of justice, is that we can have a strong sense of injustice on many different grounds, and yet not agree on one particular ground as being the dominant reason for the diagnosis of injustice. (p. 3)

For example, Sen cites the impeachment of Warren Hastings in 1788 and the US invasion of Iraq in 2003 and argues that there were many arguments for impeachment and against invasion that should be taken into account and even if a community may disagree on any one of them the arguments correctly point to the right conclusion. So, *in the theory of justice there should not be only one proof*, but many discourses to be considered.

> Arbitrary reduction of multiple and potentially conflicting principles to one solitary survivor, guillotining all the other evaluative criteria, is not, in fact, a prerequisite for getting useful and robust conclusions on what should be done. This applies as much to the theory of justice as it does to any other part of the discipline of practical reason. (p. 4)

Then Sen classifies all existing moral theories in two broad types: (1) *transcendental institutionalism*—search of perfectly just institutions (e. g. Hobbes, Kant, and Rawls) and (2) *realization-focused comparison*—discussion of current institutions and their potential improvements (e. g. Smith, Bentham, and Marx). Sen explains that his book is devoted to the second approach and answers questions like "How would justice be advanced?" rather than questions like "'What would be perfectly just institutions?" Still this analysis should bring a "radical change in the formulation of the theory of justice."

Sen is quite skeptical about the possibility of the transcendental approach to find a universal moral truth ("there may be no reasoned agreement at all, even under strict conditions of impartiality and open-minded scrutiny"). Transcendental approach assumes that there will be only on impartial approach but, according to Sen, this is may be a mistake. For example, John Rawls suggests that the universal solution is the lexicographic maximin rule, but he does not provide convincing arguments that would eliminate all other alternative impartial rules of distribution. Beside this Sen believes that in practice we need "a framework for comparison of justice for choosing among the feasible alternatives" but not a fundamental theory of an unattainable ideal.

Sen claims that a universal solution is "incurably problematic" but at the same time he does not provide a proof of that claim. This claim could be a "Sen's impossibility theorem" but in reality it remained unproved. In contrast, many scholars agreed that the choice in Rawlsian theory is essentially made by *one person* because all people in the original position should think *in the same way*. Therefore, it would be logical to assume that there should be a universal solution.

It is obvious from his book that Sen did not think that ethics might be a science. This becomes explicit when he discusses the methodology of Sidgwick (p. 118). As a result the book is quite difficult to read. Although it contains many wonderful questions, facts, and ideas, the discussion seems to be unbearably long and unproductive.

JOHN HARSANYI

A Hungarian-American economist *John Harsanyi* (1920–2000) was awarded the Nobel Prize in 1994 for his contribution to studies of games with incomplete information, or Bayesian games. This "technical" theoretical task actually had a crucial importance for the problem of choice under veil of ignorance and that is why it is not surprising that Harsanyi succeeded in making several important advances to the Rawlsian approach.

First, historically he suggested the idea of veil of ignorance a bit earlier than Rawls. In 1948 Milton Friedman and Leonard Savage declared a return to cardinal utility in the analysis of risk-taking (borrowing from Neumann and Morgenstern). Harsanyi noticed that the same approach may be applied to welfare economics and in 1953 he published a two-page note *Cardinal Utility in Welfare Economics and in the Theory of Risk-taking* where he expressed this idea. He wrote that "there is a fairly plausible interpretation of the concept of social welfare—or, more precisely, of value judgments concerning social welfare—which brings the cardinal utility concept of welfare economics very close to the cardinal utility concept used in the theory of choices involving risk" (p. 434). He defined "value judgments" as "nonegoistic impersonal judgments of preference." An "egoistic judgment" takes place when a poor person expresses a preference for increase in support. "Nonegoistic" assumes that the same preference is expressed by a rich person.

> ...a value judgment on the distribution of income would show the required impersonality to the highest degree if the person who made this judgment had to choose a particular income distribution in complete ignorance of what his own relative position (and the position of those near to his heart) would be within the system chosen. This would be the case if he had exactly the same chance of obtaining the first position (corresponding to the highest income) or the second or the third, etc., up to the last position (corresponding to the lowest income) available within that scheme. (pp. 434–435)

This definition makes impersonal preference judgments very similar to choice involving risk because the actor does not know his place in the society. However, that paper only emphasized this opportunity and did not add anything else to this idea.

Second, when in 1971 John Rawls published his *Theory of Justice* as a new contractarian approach that should replace Utilitarianism, Harsanyi disagreed with the maximin criterion. Beside this Harsanyi thought that Utilitarianism remains the most reasonable, clear, systematic, and rational concept of morality and wrote a paper *Can the Maximin Principle Serve as a Basis for Morality* (1975) to prove that the Rawlsian suggestion to dismantle Utilitarianism cannot succeed. The point of criticism was the decision rule which was assumed by Rawls—maximin rule. This principle of choice under uncertainty was popular in 1930–1940s, but since mid of 1950s it became clear that maximin sometimes leads to curious outcomes and it should be replaced with expected utility maximization approach. For example, according to Rawls' original position, we should always give preference to the worst-off people regardless of the sacrifice of other people. Harsanyi provides an example with extremely expensive treatment for one retarded individual which would improve his condition only slightly but would cost the education of many able young people. This choice is moral according to maximin strategy, but it is not according to Utilitarianism and common sense (which is used by Harsanyi as a foundation for moral theory). Therefore we should replace maximin with expected utility maximization. Under veil of ignorance any actor will vote not for spending all resources for the retarded person but for a more balanced distribution of resources among all young people. It was not refutation of veil of ignorance approach but just replacing one criterion with another. (Remember the similar example by Nozick.)

Interestingly, Harsanyi claims that his theory is utilitarian compared to a contractarian approach of Rawls.

> While Rawls's approach yields a moral theory in the contractarian tradition, my own model yields a moral theory based on the principle of average utility and, therefore, clearly belonging to the utilitarian tradition. (p. 598)

This claim is correct, because maximizing expected individual utility by every actor under veil of ignorance is the same as maximizing total utility. However, a more correct conclusion would be that the scientific moral theory integrates utilitarian and contractarian ideas.

In 1977 Harsanyi wrote the paper *Morality and the Theory of Rational Behavior* which made a huge step toward building a scientific moral theory. He viewed ethics as a branch of the general theory of rational behavior but a special type of this behavior dealing with norms choice. His purpose was to prove that there is a "unique rational answer" to the philosophical question "What is morality?" He claimed that answering this question we can obtain "a very specific decision rule for choosing between alternative possible moral codes."

He suggested the "equiprobability model for moral judgments" which should be the basis of moral theory. Essentially this theory reproduced "veil of ignorance" because it assumed the choice of a moral code without knowing in advance what particular social position one would occupy in the society. However, according to decision theory an individual will maximize not the utility of the worst positions but expected utility. If there are n positions in the society and there is a vector of utilities at every position U_1, U_2, ..., U_n, the individual will maximize the expected utility W_i.

$$W_i = \frac{1}{n}\sum_{j=1}^{n} U_j$$

It is assumed that the individual can anticipate its utility at any position through a thought experiment. This assumption is called a *similarity postulate* and essentially offers a solution for interpersonal comparison of utilities (a fundamental problem of welfare economics).

Moreover, in this paper, Harsanyi makes a couple of additional important assumptions which are very close to our version of scientific moral theory. First, Harsanyi assumes that we should exclude from moral norms' choice individuals with "antisocial preferences." Second, Harsanyi assumes that an individual may be wrong about his preferences because of knowledge shortage. He calls the observed choice of a person "manifest preferences" and his real choice "true preferences."

> a person's true preferences are the preferences he would have if he had all the relevant factual information, always reasoned with the greatest possible care, and were in a state of mind most conducive to rational choice.

All these arguments were very useful to pave the road to a scientific approach in ethics.

DAVID GAUTHIER

Canadian-American philosopher *David Gauthier* (born 1932) was attracted to ethics after reading *Language of Morals* by R. M. Hare even though Gauthier disagreed with Hare on many issues. In 1961 Gauthier defended his doctoral thesis on moral theory which was later published in an abridged form under the title *Practical Reasoning* (1963). In this book he claimed that a moral theory ("practical reasoning" in his terms) should operate similar to a science, because it predicts what a rational man should do to achieve his purposes.

Just as the philosopher of science seeks to set out the conditions of scientific inference, so we have attempted to state the supreme condition of practical inference. Appraisal based on this condition relates to what: we may call the methodology of practice. It, too, is comparable on the one hand to logical appraisal in its concern with reasoning, but, on the other hand, is directly related to practice, just as is appraisal of the agent's capacity to effect his judgements in his decisions and actions. Failure to adopt the correct standards of judgement, just as failure to act in accordance with judgement, opens the door to the charges 'imprudent' and 'immoral'.

Methodological considerations do not, of course, determine the truth of proposed scientific theories—only their relation to the facts to be explained can do this. And similarly, methodological considerations do not determine the truth of particular practical judgements—only their relation to the agent's situation and the interests therein involved can do this. In giving an account of practical reasoning, the philosopher is not doing the job of the man faced with a practical problem, any more than, in giving an account of scientific reasoning, he is doing the job of the scientist. The philosopher does not pre-determine practical or scientific conclusions. Rather, he reflects upon, and makes clear, what the rational agent and the rational inquirer must do, to succeed in the tasks they set themselves. (7.1. The Condition of Practical Inference)

And one more citation.

The conclusions of scientific arguments, whether they be statements explaining the data set out in the premises, or statements predicting occurrences by extrapolation from the data, are capable at least of independent check. The prediction may be verified by observing the occurrence; the explanation may be confirmed by applying it to further data. In this way the truth of the conclusions can be used to assess the validity of the methods of argument.

> There is a partial parallel with practical arguments. The conclusion of an argument, a judgement about what action is to be done, may be checked by observing the effects of doing the action. Ilk does best satisfy the wants of the persons concerned, then it is what one ought to have done, and hence the practical judgement is true. (7.1.1. Validity)

In the late 1960s Gauthier discovered Prisoners Dilemma and during the next several years worked on rethinking "practical reasoning" with an account for this new model (Gauthier 1967, 1969, 1977). In 1985 he published the book *Moral by Agreements* which summarized his research during previous years. He wrote in the preface that initially he did not plan to offer this framework as a moral theory to persuade everyone but just as a set of theoretical contemplations, but at the moment of finishing the book he decided that this claim can be made.

> What theory of morals, we might better ask, can ever serve any useful purpose, unless it can show that all the duties it recommends are also truly endorsed in each individual's reason? If moral appeals are entitled to some practical effect, some influence on our behaviour, it is not because they whisper invitingly to our desires, but because they convince our intellect.

In the beginning he writes that a good moral theory should start with a methodology of proper normative reasoning, but he will not do this and proceed with building the theory.

> A complete philosophy of morals would need to explain, and perhaps to defend, the idea of a normative theory. We shall not do this. But we shall exemplify normative theory by sketching the theory of rational choice. Indeed, we shall do more. We shall develop a theory of morals as part of the theory of rational choice. We shall argue that the rational principles for making choices, or decisions among possible actions, include some that constrain the actor pursuing his own interest in an impartial way. These we identify as moral principles.

Probably as a result of this methodological negligence the book is quite difficult to read. In many cases it is not even clear if the author is using positive or normative rhetoric. For example, this is a rather important fragment discussing morality of free market. Is it positive or normative analysis?

Morality arises from market failure. The first step in making this claim good is to show that the perfect market, were it realized, would constitute a morally free zone, a zone within which the constraints of morality would have no place. In leaving each person free to pursue her own interest in her own way, the market satisfies the ideal of moral anarchy. (*IV: The Market: Freedom from Morality*)

Therefore, does morality arise from market failure in reality or ought it? Would the perfect market constitute a morally free zone in reality or ought it? Such a confusion of positive and normative argumentation is not very productive.

Another methodological problem of Gauthier's analysis is careless use of terminology. As a result we may observe a number of vague propositions which may be easily dismissed as incorrect or simply wrong. For example,

Where market interaction, with its pre-established harmony between equilibrium and optimum, is beyond good and evil, and natural interaction, in the presence of free-riders and parasites, degenerates into force and fraud, co-operative interaction is the domain of justice. (*V. Co-operation: bargaining and Justice*, paragraph 2)

How can a harmony be "beyond good and evil" if it is good for people according to Gauthier's argument? What do these terms "good" and "evil" mean to make this proposition meaningful?

In Chap. 4 Gauthier describes a framework with perfect competition and its distortions which require regulation (market power, externalities, and public goods) which is very appropriate for economic or business ethics, but is it applicable to general ethics? The title of the book suggests that it is a general moral theory but the framework is focused on economic moral issues. Does Gauthier assume that its conclusions are applicable for general ethics? It remains unclear.

In the next chapter Gauthier develops a bargaining theory which essentially belongs to game theory and not to ethics. He develops an interesting model of "minimax relative concession" which assumes that every party in win-lose bargaining will try to minimize its relative loss comparing to the other party losses. This result does not look very persuasive even in economic theory, but it is far from explaining behavior in a huge variety of real life moral issues. Besides this, it is not a normative theory, but a positive theory of constrained maximization. Can Gauthier prove that this type of behavior is a moral one? He does not try to do this. A similar criticism of "minimax relative concession" for lacking moral foundation was provided Gregory Kavka (1987).

> Is minimax relative concession a fair solution to the problem of distributing the cooperative surplus? We may doubt this because of the role of maximal claims in determining relative shares. Imagine an Inequality Glutton who would derive much utility from having much larger shares than others of the material components of the cooperative surplus. Because of his psychology, his maximum claim would correspond to a much higher share of the material benefits of cooperation than would the maximum claim of those who have little or no preference for having much more than others. Equal relative concessions from the Inequality Glutton will leave him with many more material benefits than most others-because he starts from a higher (in terms of level or share of material benefits) claim point. In general, distribution to achieve minimax relative concession most rewards those who most prefer material inequality and punishes those who would be satisfied with an equal share. This hardly seems like justice or the outcome of a fair bargain. (p. 119)

THOMAS SCANLON

An American philosopher *Thomas Scanlon* (born 1940) made a significant advance in scientific variant of ethics. Having a philosophical background he wrote a dissertation on mathematical logic and proof theory, so one might assume that the culture of precise and strict theorizing should have a serious influence on his writings in ethics. Scanlon was also influenced by John Rawls as a PhD student in Harvard. As a result Scanlon indeed came very close to a scientific approach to ethics.

First, in his paper *Contractualism and Utilitarianism* (1982) Scanlon announced the idea to reconsider the nature of moral theory. He suggested that such a moral theory should be able to justify one's actions to others on grounds that *they could not reasonably reject*—this principle will be central in all his later works. He made several important steps to move ethics closer to science, even though it also was his explicit task. In the first pages he even promoted analogy between ethics and mathematics, suggesting that both disciplines are interesting in finding proof but in both cases the truth is inevitably conventional in character.

There is such a subject as moral philosophy for much the same reason that there is such a subject as the philosophy of mathematics. In moral judgments, as in mathematical ones, we have a set of putatively objective beliefs in which we are inclined to invest a certain degree of confidence and importance. Yet on reflection it is not at all obvious what, if anything, these judgments can be about, in virtue of which some can be said to be correct or defensible and others not. This question of subject matter, or the grounds of truth, is the first philosophical question about both morality and mathematics. Second, in both morality and mathematics it seems to be possible to discover the truth simply by thinking or reasoning about it. Experience and observation may be helpful, but observation in the normal sense is not the standard means of discovery in either subject. So, given any positive answer to the first question–any specification of the subject matter or ground of truth in mathematics or morality–we need some compatible epistemology explaining how it is possible to discover the facts about this subject matter through something like the means we seem to use.

In this paper Scanlon discussed many important issues about the methodology of this proof. For example, Scanlon discussed the question who should be included into the number of actors who define moral norms.

The general specification of the scope of morality which it implies seems to me to be this: morality applies to a being if the notion of justification to a being of that kind makes sense. What is required in order for this to be the case? Here I can only suggest some necessary conditions. The first is that the being has a good, that is, that there be a clear sense in which things can be said to go better or worse for that being. This gives partial sense to the idea of what it would be reasonable for a trustee to accept on the being's behalf. It would be reasonable for a trustee to accept at least those things that are good, or not bad, for the being in question. Using this idea of trusteeship we can extend the notion of acceptance to apply to beings that are incapable of literally agreeing to anything.

However, this discussion was not very systematic and the purpose was not to lay down a comprehensive methodology but to clarify some contemporary methodological disputes between contractualism with Utilitarianism.

Like Rawls, Scanlon did not distinguish between positive and normative analysis and it seems that this factor made his task unsolvable. Strictly speaking, "reflective equilibrium" is about positive analysis and it is not a normative theory. It is true that "some people may disagree" but why should a scientific investigation verify its hypotheses by the opinion of "some people"?

In his book *What We Owe to Each Other* (1998) Scanlon continued to develop a moral theory based on the principle that "everyone ought to follow the principles that no one could reasonably reject."

> An act is wrong if and only if any principle that permitted it would be one that could reasonably be rejected by people moved to find principles for the general regulation of behaviour that others, similarly motivated, could not reasonably reject. (p. 4)

In the introduction he suggested that this is a separate domain of moral theory called "what we owe to each other," and it is described in the third part of the book. Scanlon starts the book with a long discussion of *reasons* which looks like a clarification of terminology (reason, rationality, irrationality, desires, motives, etc.) and elaboration of a model of man. Finally he asks such questions as "how do we know what reasons we have." This analysis looks like another "treatise on human nature" but is it necessary for developing a moral theory? Only some of these clarifications looks relevant. For example, Scanlon suggests that although people may disagree about reasons, some of them can be *mistaken about their reasons* for action, and "not just mistaken about what will promote their ends, but mistaken in having those ends to begin with."

The next two chapters are devoted to a similar discussion of *values* and *well-being*. It is again not clear if a new moral theory really needs this clarification. This is not a new theory of morality but only a preliminary discussion of various conceptual issues that come to the mind of a contemporary philosopher in this regard.

Scanlon claims that his approach differs from Kant, Gauthier, or Rawls, but his contradictions with their framework are not clear. Kant derives universal moral norms as norms which one could rationally will to hold as universal laws, but it means that one does not have reasons for rejecting these moral laws. Rawls derives moral norms by using veil of ignorance but if this is a good principle then one should have reason to disagree with that. Gauthier assumes that agreement about norms is based on rational strategy to increase welfare, but again no one should have reason to disagree with that.

Scanlon insists that his approach is more about "reasonableness rather than rationality" in their approaches. By "rationality" he understands pursuing one's goals. By "reasonableness" he understands a deeper notion of rationality that includes reassessment of long-term aims. It is better for a person to be reasonable than rational.

In this book Scanlon once more expresses the idea that ethics should be a science and said that it is a "practical discipline" telling us what we should do.

> This is because, in contrast to everyday empirical judgments, scientific claims, and religious beliefs that involve claims about the origin and control of the universe, the point of judgments of right and wrong is not to make claims about what the spatiotemporal world is like. The point of such judgments is, rather, a practical one: they make claims about what we have reason to do. Metaphysical questions about the subject matter of judgments of right and wrong are important only if answers to them are required in order to show how these judgments can have this practical significance. (p. 2)

He implicitly offers a scientific approach because he assumes possibility of proof which does not depend on subjective biases, should be based on knowledge, can be reasonably explained, and requires consent.

> It describes judgments of right and wrong as judgments about reasons and justification, judgments of a kind that can be correct or incorrect and that we are capable of assessing through familiar forms of thought that should not strike us as mysterious.

SAMUEL HARRIS VS. SEAN CARROLL

American philosopher and neuroscientist *Samuel Harris* is known as an active advocate of scientific knowledge and secular values in society. In 2011 he published the book *The Moral Landscape: How Science Can Determine Human Values*, where he suggested that there are objective facts about happiness and well-being and they can be used as a foundation of moral science. He emphasized that by moral science he understands not positive but normative ethics.

> I was not suggesting that science could give us an evolutionary or neurobiological account of what people do in the name of "morality." Nor was I merely saying that science can help us get what we want out of life. Both of these would have been quite banal claims to make (unless one happens to doubt the truth of evolution or the mind's dependency on the brain). Rather I was suggesting that science can, in principle, help us understand

what we should do and should want—and, perforce, what other people should do and want in order to live the best lives possible. My claim is that there are right and wrong answers to moral questions, just as there are right and wrong answers to questions of physics, and such answers may one day fall within reach of the maturing sciences of mind. (p. 28)

In the same year Sam Harris presented a TED talk entitled "Science Can Answer Moral Questions." The well-known cosmologist *Sean Carroll* responded to this talk with strong criticism emphasizing that Hume was right and we cannot derive *ought* from *is*. He acknowledged the objectives of pleasure and suffering but pointed to the pleasure of sadists which should not be respected so we cannot make pleasure as such the basis of moral theory.

There are not objective moral truths (where "objective" means "existing independently of human invention"), but there are real human beings with complex sets of preferences. What we call "morality" is an outgrowth of the interplay of those preferences with the world around us, and in particular with other human beings. The project of moral philosophy is to make sense of our preferences, to try to make them logically consistent, to reconcile them with the preferences of others and the realities of our environments, and to discover how to fulfill them most efficiently. Science can be extremely helpful, even crucial, in that task. (Carroll 2010a)

It is clear again that this disagreement is also about definitions. If we understand moral science as objective Utilitarianism (maximization of aggregate well-being), such a "science" is not proved. Later Carroll published one more article with more structured arguments which represented a correct scientific criticism of such Utilitarianism: there is no universal definition of well-being, no proof that it should be maximized, and it is impossible to aggregate well-being of different people and so on.

However, what about building a moral science as a theory of rational choice and consensus? Interestingly, Carroll comes close to this idea of moral science as a theory of human preferences. In another article he suggested that ethics may be developed in the same way as natural science—reaching a consensus of scholars on the basis of common methodology.

When it comes to morality, we indeed have a very similar situation. If we all agree on a set of starting moral assumptions, then we constitute a functioning community that can set about figuring out how to pass moral judgments. (Carroll 2010b)

But Carroll does not believe that it would be a universal moral truth because it depends on the "moral community." You can prove to your moral community that the Taliban is wrong but you cannot prove it to *any other* moral community (See also Carroll 2010c). This interesting discussion about the possibility of a scientific approach to ethics demonstrates that the problem is still relevant. Probably the approach of Chap. 2 may serve as a step in the right direction to resolve this problem. We can try to reach an agreement with *any rational thinking person* about basic moral concepts and norms. It is difficult but no one has proved yet that this is impossible.

Notes

1. The idea of veil of ignorance was earlier introduced by the economist John Harsanyi (see further in this chapter).

References

Carroll, Sean. 2010a. The Moral Equivalent of the Parallel Postulate. *Cosmic Variance*, March 24.
———. 2010b. Sam Harris Responds. *Cosmic Variance*, March 29.
———. 2010c. Science and Morality: You Can't Derive "Ought" from "Is." *Cosmic Variance*, May 3.
Gauthier, David P. 1967. Morality and Advantage. *The Philosophical Review* 76: 460–475.
———. 1969. *The Logic of Leviathan: The Moral and Political Theory of Thomas Hobbes.* Oxford University Press.
Gauthier, David. 1977. The Social Contract as Ideology. *Philosophy & Public Affairs* 6: 130–164.
Harris, Sam. 2011. *The Moral Landscape: How Science Can Determine Human Values.* Simon and Schuster.
Harsanyi, J. 1953. Cardinal Utility in Welfare Economics and in the Theory of Risk-Taking. *Journal of Political Economy* 61 (5): 434–435.
Harsanyi, John C. 1975. Can the Maximin Principle Serve as a Basis for Morality? A Critique of John Rawls's Theory. *American Political Science Review* 69 (2): 594–606.
———. 1977. Morality and the Theory of Rational Behavior. *Social Research* 44: 623–656.
Kavka, Gregory S. 1987. *Mind.* New Series, 96(381): 117–121.
Rawls, John. 1958. Justice as Fairness. *The Philosophical Review* 67: 164–194.

———. 1971. *A Theory of Justice*. Cambridge: Harvard University Press.

Scanlon, Thomas M. 1982. Contractualism and Utilitarianism. In *Utilitarianism and Beyond*, ed. Amartya Sen and Bernard Williams, 103–110. Cambridge: Cambridge University Press.

Scanlon, Thomas. 1998. *What We Owe to Each Other*. Harvard University Press.

Sen, Amartya. 1974. Rawls Versus Bentham: An Axiomatic Examination of the Pure Distribution Problem. *Theory and Decision* 4 (3): 301–309.

CHAPTER 7

Other Approaches

Abstract In this chapter we will take a short survey of several methodologies of normative ethics that were developed in the twentieth century. First, we will explore the frameworks that assume that normative ethics is based not on rational choice but on some other factors (emotivism, intuitionism, and prescriptivism). Then we will discuss the views of several authors about the possibility of scientific ethics (Nowell-Smith, Harman, Sayre-McCord). Finally, we will examine the development of virtue ethics which is often claimed to be a major approach to normative ethics.

Keywords Emotivism • Intuitionism • Prescriptivism • Virtue ethics • Scientific method

There were several directions of moral philosophy which closely associated morality with feelings: (1) emotivism, which assumes that moral propositions are generated by emotions and not reason, (2) intuitionism, which assumes that moral choice is conducted by intuition so we should search for moral truth in the latter, and (3) prescriptivism, which assumes that moral propositions express commands. We mentioned them briefly in Chap. 5 but now it is time to look closer and see what arguments they use to justify their methodological position and what it means from the point of view of a scientific approach to ethics.

© The Author(s) 2018   119
M. Storchevoy, *A Scientific Approach to Ethics*,
https://doi.org/10.1007/978-3-319-69113-8_7

EMOTIVISM

Emotivism appeared in the eighteenth century when David Hume claimed that moral propositions relate to facts but cannot be true or false because they are generated by our feelings. This idea was supported in the twentieth century by several representatives of logical positivism who believed that ethical statements are based on emotions and do not satisfy the verification principle of scientific knowledge.

The British philosopher *Alfred Jules Ayer* (1910–1989) was responsible for bringing the philosophy of logical positivism to Britain. After graduating from Oxford University he spent a year in Vienna University where he was influenced by scholars from the Vienna Circle. After his return to England he published the book *Language, Truth, and Logic* (1936), which was the first representation of logical positivism in English language.

Ayer applied his critical analysis to ethics and came to the conclusion that it is a poor potential candidate for scientific knowledge. He said that ethics is actually a quite heterogeneous whole that may be split into four classes of propositions: (1) propositions which express definitions of ethical terms, (2) propositions describing the phenomena of moral experience, (3) exhortations to moral virtue, and (4) ethical judgments. Unfortunately, philosophers often ignore the distinction between the four classes with the result that it is "often very difficult to tell from their works what it is that they are seeking to discover or prove" (chapter 6, paragraph 3). According to Ayer, it is only the first propositions that constitute moral philosophy. The second type of propositions should be studied by psychology or sociology, and exhortations to moral virtue are not propositions at all but commands and they do not belong to philosophy or science. What about ethical judgments? There is a subjectivist approach which defines rightness of an action as "approval of a certain person" and a utilitarian approach which justifies it in terms of pleasure or utility. If any of these approaches is correct, then ethics may be a science, because "it would follow that ethical assertions were not generically different from the factual assertions which are ordinary contrasted to them" and may be verified as other empirical hypotheses. However Ayer rejects both of them. The subjectivist approach is wrong because "some actions which are generally approved are not right," and the Utilitarianism approach is wrong because "it is sometimes wrong to perform the action which would actually or probably cause the greatest happiness." So normative ethical judgments are irreducible to empirical concepts which make them unverifiable and non-scientific.

In admitting that normative ethical concepts are irreducible to empirical concepts, we seem to be leaving the way clear for the 'absolutist' view of ethics—that is, the view that statements of value are not controlled by observation, as ordinary empirical propositions are, but only by a mysterious 'intellectual intuition'. A feature of this theory, which is seldom recognized by its advocates, is that it makes statements of value unverifiable. For it is notorious that what seems intuitively certain to one person may seem doubtful, or even false, to another. So that unless it is possible to provide some criterion by which one may decide between conflicting intuitions, a mere appeal to intuition is worthless as a test of a proposition's validity. But in the case of moral judgements no such criterion can be given. (*Language, Truth, and Logic*, p. 66)

Logically the approach of Ayer is correct but Ayer did not consider the possibility of defining moral terms in a way to make ethical judgments verifiable.

The American philosopher *Charles Leslie Stevenson* (1908–1979) graduated from Yale University with a BA in English Literature but then went to England and studied philosophy. He was strongly influenced by G. E. Moore, I. A. Richards, and L. Wittgenstein and acquired a life-long adherence to positivism. In 1937 he wrote the paper "The Emotive Meaning of Ethical Terms" which started with the same question as our scientific framework to ethics in Chap. 2.

Ethical questions first arise in the form "Is so and so good?", or "Is this alternative better than that?" These questions are difficult partly because we don't quite know what we are seeking. W e are asking, "Is there a needle in that haystack?" without even knowing just what a needle is. So the first thing to do is to examine the questions themselves. W e must try to make them clearer, either by defining the terms in which they are expressed, or by any other method that is available.

The present paper is concerned wholly with this preliminary step of making ethical questions clear. In order to help answer the question "Is X good?" we must substitute for it a question which is free from ambiguity and confusion. (p. 14)

Then he suggested that we can substitute the question "Is X good" with another question that would be better defined. He claims that the new definition should be relevant, i.e. anyone can use the new definition instead of the old one in any context where the old one was used before. Only in the case of full substitutability can we switch to a new definition.

However, if we take some variants of definition in terms of approval like "good" means "desired" (Hobbes) or "good" means "approved by most people" (Hume), we will see that they are only partially relevant. Then Stevenson provides several examples when the speaker may have some meaning in "X is good" which are lost in translation to "desired" or "approved by most" variants. For example, "good" means some "magnetism" but this rules out Humean "approved by most people" because the latter simply means a fact of approval. But moreover, "the "goodness" of anything must not be verifiable solely by use of the scientific method." Then Stevenson provided the next explanation.

> Consider, for example, the definition: "X is good" means most people would approve of X if they knew its nature and consequences. How, according to this definition, could we prove that a certain X was good? We should first have to find out, empirically, just what X was like, and what its consequences would be. To this extent the empirical method, as required by the definition, seems beyond intelligent objection. But what remains? We should next have to discover whether most people would approve of the sort of thing we had discovered X to be. This couldn't be determined by popular vote—but only because it would be too difficult to explain to the voters, beforehand, what the nature and consequences of X really were. (p. 17)

Stevenson adds that this method will be approved only by people with a democratic attitude, but aristocrats will disagree that goodness should be approved by the majority. Finally, he adds Moore's Open Question Argument.

> Mr. G. E. Moore's familiar objection about the open question is chiefly pertinent in this regard. No matter what set of scientifically knowable properties a thing may have (says Moore, in effect), you will find, on careful introspection, that it is an open question to ask whether anything having these properties is good. It is difficult to believe that this recurrent question is a totally confused one, or that it seems open only because of the ambiguity of "good". Rather, we must be using some sense of "good" which is not definable, relevantly, in terms of anything scientifically knowable. That is, the scientific method is not sufficient for ethics. (p. 18)

Then, Stevenson tries to figure out how ethical terms may be used and come to the conclusion that they are "instruments used in the complicated interplay and readjustment of human interests." One of its important functions is to bear emotive content which is also ignored by Hobbesian or Humean approaches.

In 1944 he developed this approach in a book *Ethics and Language* in which he said that ethical judgments not only express emotions but also have imperative aspect. He developed a theory of *persuasive definition*—attempts to give "a new conceptual meaning to a familiar word without substantially changing its emotive meaning, and which is used with the conscious or unconscious purpose of changing, by this means, the direction of people's interests" (1938b, 32).

Although Stevenson came very close to a scientific approach to ethics he could not resolve some difficulties and eventually rejected ethics as being scientific. Let us clarify this claim in the next arguments.

First, he did not distinguish between ordinary language and scientific terminology. Ordinary language may have many aspects and meanings of good but a scientific definition of good should not resemble all of them. The definition of "mass" in physics should not embrace all semantic variations of this word in the ordinary language.

Second, it is indeed difficult to explain to all voters the "nature and consequences" of X, but this fact does not make this method non-scientific. In many natural sciences it is difficult to measure the object of study (e.g. astronomy or nuclear physics), but they continue to be sciences and work toward the improvement of their methods. Why should ethics surrender? Moreover, in many sciences it is not necessary to measure the entire general population but enough to study a representative sample. Why should ethics not do the same?

Third, a disagreement between aristocrats and democrats is also a weak agreement. It may be the consequence of a lack of knowledge or education, because we may hypothesize that there is the best political system which will be accepted by all people. Remember, that we should use veil of ignorance (not known in 1937) if we want to achieve fairness.

Fourth, the Open Question Argument does not refute the scientific approach to ethics as it was shown in Chap. 2.

Traditions of emotivism or expressivism were continued in the second half of the twentieth century by several authors, e.g. Simon Blackburn (1993, 2006) Mark Timmons (1999).

INTUITIONISM

Intuitionism assumes that moral truth should be self-evident and does not need any arguments. The early version of intuitionism was developed in the eighteenth to nineteenth centuries by Richard Price and

Henry Sidgwick (see Chap. 3). Intuitionism was developed in the early twentieth century by British philosophers who were influenced by Moore's criticism of ethics and analytical philosophy. In 1912 an English philosopher *Harold Arthur Prichard* (1871–1947) published a paper "Does Moral Philosophy Rest on a Mistake?" where he admitted deep dissatisfaction of any student of moral philosophy which arises after studying the subject for some time. Moral philosophy is seen to be a vague discipline without clear proofs and conclusions, and there probably is a fundamental mistake in its methodology. Then Prichard offers his explanation of this situation. Prichard suggests that we always feel that we ought to act in a certain way but when this action comes into conflict with our interests we start asking ourselves if we really ought to do so. In other words we ask for proof of normative rules. All moral theories, according to Prichard, fall into two groups: (1) theories that prove that acting in this way actually leads to the person's interests or happiness and (2) theories that prove that acting in this way leads to something good. However, both approaches are illegitimate because normative statements cannot be based on non-normative axioms. In case of the first type of theories, e.g. Utilitarianism, if we prove that action is desirable or leads to the happiness of the person, we cannot prove that the action is *obligatory*. In case of the second approach, similarly, even if we prove that something is good it does not mean that we *ought* to do anything about this. Therefore, our sense of "ought" is a fundamental perception that should be accounted directly and cannot be proved or disproved by rational or other philosophical arguments.

> The sense that we ought to do certain things arises in our unreflective consciousness, being an activity of moral thinking occasioned by the various situations in which we find ourselves. At this stage our attitude to these obligations is one of unquestioning confidence. But inevitably the appreciation of the degree to which the execution of these obligations is contrary to our interest raises the doubt whether after all these obligations are, really obligatory, i.e., whether our sense that we ought not to do certain things is not illusion. We then want to have it proved to us that we ought to do so, i.e., to be convinced of this by a process which, as an argument, is different in kind from our original and unreflective appreciation of it. This demand is, as I have argued, illegitimate.
>
> Hence in the first place, if, as is almost universally the case, by Moral Philosophy is meant the knowledge which would satisfy this demand, there is no such knowledge, and all attempts to attain it are doomed to failure

because they rest on a mistake, the mistake of supposing the possibility of proving what can only be apprehended directly by an act of moral thinking. (Prichard 1912, p. 36)

This approach was criticized by Ayer who emphasized that this approach does not lead to creation of a universal moral theory, because what seems intuitively right to one person may seem intuitively wrong for another, but we do not have a criterion for comparing and evaluating these intuitions.

In admitting that normative ethical concepts are irreducible to empirical concepts, we seem to be leaving the way clear for the 'absolutist' view of ethics—that is, the view that statements of value are not controlled by observation, as ordinary empirical propositions are, but only by a mysterious 'intellectual intuition'. A feature of this theory, which is seldom recognized by its advocates, is that it makes statements of value unverifiable. For it is notorious that what seems intuitively certain to one person may seem doubtful, or even false, to another. So that unless it is possible to provide some criterion by which one may decide between conflicting intuitions, a mere appeal to intuition is worthless as a test of a proposition's validity. But in the case of moral judgements no such criterion can be given. (*Language, Truth, and Logic*, p. 66)

A deontological variant of intuitivism was developed by a Scottish philosopher *William David Ross* (1877–1971) who was famous for his translation of Aristotle and the book *The Right and The Good* (1930) which is thought to be one of the most important works of moral philosophy published in the twentieth century. Ross was deeply influenced by Prichard and Moore

Much of the book may be related to meta-ethical debates about definitions.

There is only a general presumption that since the structure of their eyes (if neither is colour-blind) is pretty much the same, the same object acting on the eyes of the two men produces pretty much the same kind of sensation. And in the case of a term like 'right', there is nothing parallel to the highly similar organization of different people's eyes, to create a presumption that when they call the same act right, they mean to refer to the same quality of it.

As a result he comes to the conclusion that there is no obvious connection between "right" and "doing the most good," because some of our promises may be prima facie duties and we should meet them regardless of the total utility. He offers several examples:

> Suppose, to simplify the case by abstraction, that the fulfilment of a promise to A would produce 1,000 units of good12 for him, but that by doing some other act I could produce 1,001 units of good for B, to whom I have made no promise, the other consequences of the two acts being of equal value; should we really think it self-evident that it was our duty to do the second act and not the first? I think not.
>
> … Or consider another phase of the same problem. If I have promised to confer on A a particular benefit containing 1,000 units of good, is it self-evident that if by doing some different act I could produce 1,001 units of good for A himself (the other consequences of the two acts being supposed equal in value), it would be right for me to do so? Again, I think not. Apart from my general *prima facie* duty to do A what good I can, I have another *prima facie* duty to do him the particular service I have promised to do him, and this is not to be set aside in consequence of a disparity of good of the order of 1,001 to 1,000 though a much greater disparity might justify me in so doing.

Therefore, Ross claims "there is no self-evident connexion between the attributes *right* and *optimific.*" This argument seems to be wrong. Sure, in the first example, the promise should be kept. Ross emphasizes that it will help to support trust which is important for… higher total utility in the future? So, does Ross base "right" on "total utility"? Moreover, in the first example the promise should be broken if we pay a compensation to A (this idea was much discussed in welfare economics in the 1930s). In the second example the promise should be broken because A would want this.

Therefore Ross suggests to build moral science not on thoughts but on "sense-experience" which should be the real data for ethics.

> It would be a mistake to found a natural science on 'what we really think', i.e. on what reasonably thoughtful and well educated people think about the subjects of the science before they have studied them scientifically. For such opinions are interpretations, and often misinterpretations, of sense-experience; and the man of science must appeal from these to sense-experience itself, which furnishes his real data. In ethics no such appeal is possible. We have no more direct way of access to the facts about rightness and goodness and about what things are right or good, than by thinking about them; the moral convictions of thoughtful and well-educated people are the data of ethics just as sense-perceptions are the data of a natural

science. Just as some of the latter have to be rejected as illusory, so have some of the former; but as the latter are rejected only when they are in conflict with other more accurate sense-perceptions, the former are rejected only when they are in conflict with other convictions which stand better the test of reflection. The existing body of moral convictions of the best people is the cumulative product of the moral reflection of many generations, which has developed an extremely delicate power of appreciation of moral distinctions; and this the theorist cannot afford to treat with anything other than the greatest respect.

As we can see, Ross came close to the scientific approach of ethics because he suggested that ethics may be a comprehensive discipline about moral truth that should be based on the opinions of people, and what is important—on well-educated people. What his framework lacks is the proper nature of intuitions (which cannot replace rational argument but represents only a biologically evolved ability for shortcuts) and a good theory of norms choice.

Ross' book was criticized and for some time interest for intuitionism weakened, but after W. V. Quine's attack on the a priori rational theories the degree of epistemological freedom increased and many scholars chose intuitionism as a promising perspective. One of the leading representatives of this perspective was *Robert Audi* who in 1996 published a paper "Intuitionism, Pluralism, and the Foundations of Ethics" aimed at reframing the epistemology of intuitionism. In 2004 Audi delivered the book *The Good in the Right* where he developed a full-scale overall intuitionist position representing a theoretical advance beyond Ross' framework. Later his framework was called "new intuitionism" (Hernandez 2011).

The problem of verification was approached by *Walter Sinnot-Armstrong* (2006, 2011) who explained it in the terms of "confirmation." Some intuitions may be considered as true but some need to be confirmed. "The basic problem of moral intuitionism starts with scientific evidence that many moral beliefs are not true" (2006, p. 15) Empirical research supports the idea that moral beliefs change with different situations of partiality, emotions, wording, framing, etc. Then Sinnot-Armstrong provided a framework of judging when a moral belief may be recognized as justified and when not, without "inferential process" or entering rational discussion on why it should be so.

Another intuitionism scholar was *Michael Huemer* who offered his framework in a nicely written book *Ethical Intuitionism* (2005) built in the traditional meta-ethical perspective. It starts with an epigraph from Albert Einstein: "The only real valuable thing is intuition." This may look like a good argument for intuitionism from the greatest scientific authority, but my intuition is that in this expression Einstein means the process of *discovery* of scientific knowledge and not providing *logical and empirical proof* of this knowledge.

Ethical intuitivism may be a good element of descriptive ethics (explaining how people shape their ethical opinions) or practical ethics (to teach real people how to make hard decisions), but not for normative ethics.

PRESCRIPTIVISM

Richard Mervyn Hare (1919–2002) in the book *The Language of Morals* (1952) provides analysis of ethics as a "logical study of the language of morals" and his main idea is that moral propositions do not *describe* anything but *prescribe* an action. He starts with the simplest form of prescriptive language, "ordinary imperative sentence," e.g. "Shut the door" and claims that much of the fundamental problems of ethical theory may be studied and resolved on this example. Then he studies "universal imperative sentences" and the reasons why people agree with or deny them. After this he studies "value-judgments" which are nor prescriptive in nature but have words like "good" or "ought" in them. So, his general typology of moral language propositions is shown in Table 7.1.

The book explores a lot of linguistic issues (e.g. how we can rethink and reformulate some simple commands like "Shut the door") but at the same time it comes very close to the scientific approach to ethics when it seeks to achieve two purposes: (1) accuracy in terminology and propositions and (2) justification of "moral imperatives." For example, in the chapter 3, "Inference," Hare examines principles which are used to prove imperatives (i.e. the central problem of scientific ethics). Hare agrees with Hume and Moore about the impossibility of deriving "ought" from "is." He claims that pure deductive reasoning can lead to a meaningful imperative

Table 7.1 Structure of moral language (Hare 1952)

Prescriptive language			
Imperatives		Value-judgments	
Singular	Universal	Non-moral	Moral

only if there is an imperative laid down in the very first premise. He refers to a general idea that in any science pure Cartesian logic cannot lead to any valuable conclusions without observations of matters of facts.

> ... a Cartesian procedure, either in science or in morals, is doomed from the very start. If any science is intended to give us conclusions of substance about matters of fact, then, if its method is deductive, these conclusions must be implicit in the premises.

Therefore, Hare tries to prove the "impossibility of a 'Cartesian' moral system" using several arguments. First, in many ethical theories an accurate logical analysis is applied to derive conclusions from a basic imperative premise which is thought to be self-evident. However, according to Hare, there are no self-evident moral axioms. For example, it is often very difficult to say should the person tell the truth in a particular situation because there may be many complicating factors. But if it is difficult for a particular situation, it is simply impossible for a general rule that will be applied to "innumerable circumstances whose details were totally unknown to us."

Second, what does it mean that the first principle is self-evident? If such a principle is to be in some sense impossible to reject, it can be for one of two reasons. First, it is self-contradictory to reject it, but in this case the principle is analytic and does not have any content and cannot tell us to do one thing rather than another. Second, its rejection was a "psychological impossibility" but then it depends on individual psychological capabilities because what one person cannot reject, the other (more sophisticated or strong) person can reject without problems. So, "impossibility to reject" is a wrong criterion.

Third, we may say that it might be not rational to reject the first principle. But what is "rational"? It may be a factual question or a question of value. If it is a purely factual question, then we cannot get imperative conclusions out of factual premises such as "so-and-so is rational." If it is a question of value, then the answer to it is self-evident in some sense in which case again our criterion of self-evidence would be circular.

Although Hare's framework brought up many interesting issues, it was generally a movement in the wrong direction. First, normative moral theory should not study the moral language of ordinary people; it is the task of descriptive ethics. Normative moral theory should explore how ordinary people should behave and what language they should have. Second,

Hare's claims that "description is not and never can be prescription" is true only until we build normative ethics on subjective individual choice and make the first definitions (like "good is what one wants to exist") in a way which makes all arguments stated inapplicable. The normative theory may be *description of prescription* without any contradictions.

Nowell-Smith

There are several examples when moral philosophers explicitly raised the question about possibility of developing moral theory as a science, but the general conclusion was almost always negative. Let us overview some of these discussions.

Patrick Horace Nowell-Smith (1914–2006) in his book *Ethics* (1954) devoted the entire chapter 4, "The Analogy between Ethics and Science," to the scientific status of ethics. He claims that any part of philosophy that achieved significant progress in providing definite answers for its questions becomes a "science" (e.g. physics). However, this is hardly possible in the case of ethics. Why? According to Nowell-Smith, moral philosophy deals with two types of questions: "what is good" and "how to achieve this." He believes that the second type of question can be answered with a high degree of accuracy (e.g. with the help of psychology), but the first question requires personal choice and is not a matter of expertise (i.e. cannot be a science). Moreover, many problems of the second type actually represent moral dilemmas (choice between two ends) and again requires personal choice ("no 'science' can help a person solve this problem; one has to discover which of these two complex states one really wants," p. 16). Perhaps it is possible to develop a scientific answer for questions about ends?

> Why cannot we discover a body of general moral truths that would help us to solve particular moral problems in the way that geometrical truths help the surveyor and mechanical truths help the engineer to solve their practical problems? Some philosophers have thought it possible to discover such truths. (Nowell-Smith 1954, p. 16)

However, the problem is that we cannot develop an accurate measurement of ends. Classical Utilitarianism tried to do this but failed because pleasure turned out to be immeasurable. Beside this, Nowell-Smith said that deriving norms from facts "must be illegitimate reasoning, since the conclusion of an argument can contain nothing which is not in the premises, and there are no 'oughts' in the premises" (Nowell-Smith 1954, p. 37). Still, Nowell-Smith agrees that there is a progress in moral philosophy because "some of these problems were solved very early in the history of mankind," and "a few fundamental rules of conduct that have never changed and probably never will."

Gilbert Harman

An attempt to rethink methodological foundation of ethics was conducted by Gilbert Harman in his book *The Nature of Morality* (1977). In the introduction to this book he claimed that meta-ethical literature turned out to be very controversial and led to incoherent results which eventually made the whole discipline uninteresting. After the 1960s philosophers started to reject using meta-ethical baggage and stopped considering meta-ethics a real methodology of ethics. He also stated that textbooks of ethics "pretend to set out a number of philosophical positions in a neutral way, letting the reader decide between them" which create a "misleading impression of philosophy" (p. ix).

Harman emphasizes the role of observation in testing ethical theories. He asks the very same question in the beginning: "Can moral principles be tested and confirmed in the way scientific principles can?" (Harman 1977, p. 3). However, his answer is negative because all our observations of moral facts are "theory laden," and they are generated in our mind on the basis of our social and educational background.

> Consider a physicist making an observation to test a scientific theory. Seeing a vapor trail in a cloud chamber, he thinks, "There goes a proton." Let us suppose that this is an observation in the relevant sense, namely, an immediate judgment made in response to the situation without any conscious reasoning having taken place. Let us also suppose that his observation confirms his theory, a theory that helps give meaning to the very term "proton" as it occurs in his observational judgment. (p. 6)

However, it is not the same with moral observations because there are no moral "protons" in reality. The idea of moral "proton" (good and evil) is constructed in the human mind, so moral observations can report only the observer but not reality. Therefore, moral theory cannot be verified with observation.

Observational evidence plays a part in science it does not appear to play in ethics, because scientific principles can be justified ultimately by their role in explaining observations, in the second sense of observation—by their explanatory role. Apparently, moral principles cannot be justified in the same way. It appears to be true that there can be no explanatory chain between moral principles and particular observings in the way that there can be such a chain between scientific principles and particular observings. Conceived as an explanatory theory, morality, unlike science, seems to be cut off from observation. (p. 9)

Geoffrey Sayre-McCord

An American philosopher *Geoffrey Sayre-McCord* in the paper "Coherentist epistemology and moral theory" (1996) asked a similar question: "Under what conditions are a person's moral beliefs epistemically justified?" He suggested a "coherent theory of justification" which seems to him very similar to scientific methodology.

The process is at least analogous to the one we rely on in developing our scientific theories, where we start with various observations, hypotheses, and hunches and then work to bring these together within a coherent system. All the while, we are adjusting the theoretical principles so as to fit the relevant observations, articulate the general hypotheses, and follow our hunches, even as we are refining our observations, altering our hypotheses, and reevaluating our hunches, to bring them in line with our best theories. (1996, pp. 141–142)

The person starts with the "attitudes, convictions, and beliefs" she has and then tries to remove all inconsistencies between particular moral propositions and general moral claims, articulating principles that are already implicit in the judgments, and seeking out further grounds that would justify and unify these judgments and principles, always willing to shift one's view in light of the developments. As a result, there might be two "reflective" equilibria.

Two sorts of equilibria might be sought in moral theorizing: a narrow equilibrium that is reached if one settles on a set of moral principles that cohere well with the moral judgments that, on reflection, one is willing to embrace; and a wider equilibrium that requires more, as it brings into the mix not just particular moral judgments and general moral principles but also judgments and principles concerning whatever psychological, social, physical, or meta-physical matters might prove relevant—including judgments and principles about the relevance of these other areas. (p. 142)

Unfortunately, the only focus of this scientific analogy is removing inconsistency, which is obviously important, but how can we say that a person's "coherent moral theory" is truly moral? After some contemplation Sayre-McCord comes to a relativist position, assuming that "epistemologically justified" positions of various people can differ and we cannot do anything with this.

A person might be epistemically justified in holding her beliefs, and yet be holding beliefs that are morally abhorrent, just as with more mundane matters a person might justifiably believe what turns out to be false. Needless to say, a person who holds abhorrent beliefs will; in an important sense, not be holding the beliefs she should. Worse, she might, on the basis of those beliefs, act in deeply objectionable ways. But the grounds we have for thinking her actions immoral and her views horribly mistaken might (sadly) be unavailable to her; and if they are unavailable to her, and we recognize this, we may have to grant that she is epistemically justified in holding her position. (p. 148)

VIRTUE ETHICS

Virtue ethics is often considered one of the three main approaches to normative ethics. Its ideas were expressed by many ancient philosophers but the fullest exposition was provided by Aristotle in *Nicomachean Ethics*. In this tradition the main purpose of human life was *eudemonia* which may be approximately translated as "flourishing." A person achieves eudemonia if one develops an excellent character consisting from *virtues*—traits or qualities that are morally good and lead to good moral being. Aristotle suggested an elaborated theory of virtues based on the idea of the golden mean (most qualities become virtues when they reach a position between two extremes).

During the Enlightenment, interest in Aristotle's ethics of virtues was virtually lost in connection with the development of new ethical theories—Utilitarianism and Deontology, which were more in line with the spirit of rationalism and the rejection of religious ideology.

However, in the middle of the twentieth century the situation began to change, when some philosophers started to disagree with the dominance of very abstract moral theories. In 1958, the British philosopher *Elizabeth Anscombe* in her article "Modern Moral Philosophy" sharply criticized the achievements of the ethics of the eighteenth and nineteenth centuries. She wrote that Hume confused the is-ought problem which is not as simple as it seems at first glance, and generally fell into sophistry. Utilitarianism was criticized for its obsession with utility. Kant was criticized for the individualistic approach to norms derivation although it is a business of community. The main problem of these approaches was that they placed too much emphasis on the concepts of "moral norm" and "moral duty." Anscombe pointed to the fact that Aristotle did not have any notions of "duty" or "norm." These concepts appeared in the era of Christianity, which took them from the Old Testament given by the main moral legislator. A similar concept was held by the Stoics. During the Enlightenment, philosophy was freed from the dogmas of Christianity but the concept of "moral law" was used simply by inertia. As a result, a "legal conception of ethics" appeared. However, how is this possible if the main moral legislator is gone? According to Anscombe, this is a methodological error. Ethics needs to be freed again from the quasi-legal terminology and return to the old Aristotelian tradition that will study what exists in reality—a person, his character, his desires, etc. We cannot build ethics until we do not properly master moral psychology.

Anscombe suggested an interesting view on the development of the methodology of moral philosophy although her argument was not perfect—it is unclear why the place of main moral legislator cannot be occupied by people and why ethics should study moral norms. However, Anscombe made a strong impact on philosophers and was responsible for a revival of interest to virtue ethics in the second half of the twentieth century.

In 1976 Michael Stocker published the paper "The schizophrenia of modern ethical theories" where he claimed that "one mark of a good life is a harmony between one's motives and one's reasons, values, justification," but there is serious conflict between motives and duties in contemporary ethical theories that makes people unhappy. People are taught by moral philosophy to act from duty instead of to act from love and internal motives.

One of the most famous supporters of the ethics of virtue was a Scottish philosopher *Alasdair MacIntyre* (b.1929) who published, in 1981, the book *After Virtue* which became one of the most influential works in virtue ethics in the twentieth century. MacIntyre claimed that modern ethical thought was in crisis. Enlightenment philosophers tried to find a single basis for morality, but in the end they could not come to an agreement. Philosophers appeal to abstract moral principles, but their appeals appear eclectic, inconsistent, and incoherent. As a consequence, such approaches as emotivism or skepticism have developed, which are also erroneous. Philosophy has turned into discussion of moral language and mastering moral rhetoric to manipulate others in defense of the arbitrary choices of its users. According to MacIntyre, the only correct way out of this situation is to return to the more holistic ethics of Aristotle and his concepts of man and meaning of life.

MacIntyre offered his version of virtue ethics based on the concept of *practice*—a complex human activity. Any practice has its own standards of excellence, which helps to understand how well a person performs this practice. Examples of practice are any professional activity, sport, music, science, etc. Practice can bring a person *external goods*—money, honor, career—or *internal goods* and the pleasure of the practice itself as well as the achievement of a high level of skill in this practice. Virtues (e.g., patience, accuracy, etc.) are necessary for a person to obtain internal goods from the practices that they are engaged in.

> A virtue is an acquired human quality the possession and exercise of which tends to enable us to achieve those goods which are internal to practices and the lack of which effectively prevents us from achieving any such goods. (MacIntyre, *After Virtue*, p. 191)
>
> The aim internal to such productive crafts, when they are in good order, is never only to catch fish, or to produce beef or milk, or to build houses. It is to do so in a manner consonant with the excellences of the craft, so that there is not only a good product, but the craftsperson is perfected through and in her or his activity. (MacIntyre 1985, p. 284)

MacIntyre makes a contrast between *institutions* (aimed at external goods) and *practices* (aimed at internal goods). Institutions are evil because they have "competitiveness" and "acquisitiveness" but practices are good. MacIntyre provides an example of two fishing crews. One is motivated solely by external goods—wages for the crew and profit for the owners. If they find a more profitable occupation, they will leave their profession. The second crew is focused on internal goods and seeks the excellence required by the practice of fishing; the economic side of this activity is of secondary importance.

The main problem of new virtue ethics is its *confusing methodological status*. Virtue ethics was proposed as an alternative for other approaches as Utilitarianism or Deontology, but it was not. Many sources even claim that it is a normative alternative (Stanford Encyclopedia of Philosophy).

The introduction by guest editors to the special issue of *Business Ethics Quarterly* in 2012 started with the claim that "virtue ethics takes the view that right action is defined by reference to the virtues, not vice versa, and, in particular, not primarily by reference to principles" (Sison et al. 2012).

This is a completely unwise solution according to the scientific approach to ethics. It was shown by Mill (see Chap. 3) that there is no contradiction between virtues and utility and it is strange that his voice is ignored by contemporary virtue philosophers.

In reality, virtue ethics was indeed a good alternative for moral philosophers who chose a direction of academic work in the situation where there was intense competition of talents and topics in the philosophical market. But scholars who chose virtue ethics mistakenly decided that virtue ethics is an alternative to other traditions.

There is a place for virtue ethics in the scientific ethics, but to understand it we should carefully distinguish normative, positive, and practical theories. Let us examine them one by one.

Normative ethical theory. We can rewrite the normative analysis in the language of virtues. The main question would be "What character should develop an actor?" instead of "What action is good?" Then we could render the same sequence of questions which will lead us to the same outcome but clothed in virtue terminology: "Any person should have personal freedom to develop moral character as one wants as long as it does not prevent other people to do the same and has all available information." All available information in this case includes the teachings of Aristotle and contemporary virtue ethics and all other sciences. Should we say instead "Any person should develop an excellence in character"? It seems that we should not because it would be similar to "Any person should be happy." All normal people would like to be happy and develop excellence in character without our requests because, as Aristotle and MacIntyre suggested, internal reward is a very valuable thing. Probably, some people even after having all available information will find this unattractive and will shape their life purpose using different concepts. Should we make them out to be virtuous as the majority want and Aristotle-MacIntyre suggest? A scientific answer is no.

Positive ethical theory. We can study the human character on the basis of psychology, sociology, and evolutionary economics. Various capabilities to experience feelings and intuitions may be a product of biological and social evolution (see Chap. 2). We can explain why man has these capabilities and how they work. Assumptions of Hutcheson, Hume, and others about adaptation of human character for practical purposes were confirmed by psychology and experimental economics. Moreover they study not only normal virtuous behavior or extra virtuous behavior but also vice behavior (psychopaths or sociopaths). Should we call this research virtue ethics? Probably, philosophers now can take this result and make some generalization but it seems that these generalizations will not belong to positive analysis but rather to the normative or practical genre.

Practical ethical theory. We can develop a practical approach to develop excellence in people's character. It could be some programs for school and university education as well as some coaching and training for adults (including recommendation for family education of children). Probably, it would be more effective if we render the trainings *in the language of virtues*. It looks natural because we have a ready terminology of virtues and the power of world literature (fiction). It would be great even for changing the behavior of business people who may be unaware of abstract philosophical categories but understand the right traits of a businessman's character (e.g., about caring, saving, perseverance).

Some of these ideas were proposed by various scholars. For example, *Eugene Sadler-Smith* in his paper "Before Virtue: Biology, Brain, Behavior, and the Moral Sense" (2012) supported "the need for a scientific account of virtue" on the basis of psychological and economic approaches but suggested that these approaches *do not substitute* virtue ethics. The paper offers many interesting citations and thoughts but eventually Sadler-Smith did not suggest an appropriate division of labor for these disciplines. It seems that he could not do this because he did not distinguish between normative, positive, and practical dimensions and talked about some general "virtue ethics."

The idea of practical application of virtue ethics was suggested by *Robert Solomon* in his article "Corporate Roles, Personal Virtues: An Aristotelean Approach to Business Ethics" (1992) which drew attention to the fact that in the ethics of business training there is an eclectic mix of approaches (Utilitarianism, natural rights theory, Kant, Rawls, etc.), and all these theories are very abstract and divorced from business. Accordingly, businessmen and managers, for whom these books are written, find it extremely difficult to understand them or to apply them. Against this background, the more ancient ethics of Aristotle's virtues offers a much more attractive perspective, since it is much easier for businessmen and managers to talk about the right traits of a businessman's character (e.g., about caring, saving, perseverance) than about abstract theories. In addition, according to Solomon, education of the right kind always precedes the formulation or application of principles. Solomon proposed using the Aristotelian concept of virtues and good-nature education, which is harmonious, simple, and can be successfully promoted in business. Subsequently, Solomon developed this idea in other articles, and also brought this concept to the active attention of other researchers who tried to supplement and refine his approach [Forsyth 1992; Brewer 1997; Limbs and Fort 2000].

Compatibility of virtue ethics with rational theories of ethics was supported by Raymond Devettere in *Introduction to Virtue Ethics* (2002) ("Virtue never conflicts with a person's self-interest, rightly understood"). But Devettere bases his theory mostly on ancient theories and shows no interest in building a unifying approach.

Christine Swanton in her book *Virtue Ethics: A Pluralistic View* (2003) develops virtue ethics as an alternative approach to normative and descriptive ethics and consciously does not want to compare it to rival approaches.

> To be taken seriously as a separate kind of moral theory, virtue ethics must offer its own virtue-centred conceptions of fundamental moral ideas: the modes and bases of moral response (as they feature in virtue), objectivity, the demandingness of ethics, practice, rightness of actions, 'maximizing' or 'satisficing' conceptions of ethics. In this book I spend considerably more time in this endeavour than in arguing for the superiority of virtue ethics over its rivals. (p. 6)

However, why should a philosopher develop a new framework if it is not superior to the existing ones?

Justin Oakley and Dean Cocking in their book *Virtue Ethics and Professional Roles* (2001) also try to defend virtue ethics as an alternative to consequentialism and Deontology. They introduce a new concept of "regulatory ideal."

To say that an agent has a regulative ideal is to say that they have inter-nalised a certain conception of correctness or excellence, in such a way that they are able to adjust their motivation and conduct so that it conforms—or at least does not conflict—with that standard. So, for instance, a man who has internalised a certain conception of what it is to be a good father can be guided by this conception in his practices as a father, through regu-lating his motivations and actions towards his children so that they are consistent with his conception of good fathering. A regulative ideal is thus an internalised normative disposition to direct one's actions and alter one's motivation in certain ways. Principles of normative theories, the standards of excellence embodied in the virtues, a conception of friend-ship, standards of excellence in a musical genre, or principles of grammar in a natural language could all function as regulative ideals in various agents' psychologies. (p. 25)

Oakley and Cocking write that regulative ideals of normal people include some human goods like love and friendship. Consequentialism and Kantian ethics fail to recognize the value of these things, but this may be done using virtue ethics which has some superiority over the former. From the scientific point of view this is a confusion of normative and posi-tive analysis. "Regulatory ideal" is a concept from descriptive ethics or moral psychology, but consequentialism and Deontology are normative approaches. Oakley and Cocking wanted to show that virtue ethics is an excellent model for practical ethics and may be effectively applied in rela-tionships between doctors and patients (as they do in Chaps. 4–6). However, it was not necessary to claim that virtue ethics is better than consequentialism or Deontology but simply to suggest, as Robert Solomon did (see above), that for practical purposes the language of virtues works better than the language of utility or duty.

Stan van Hooft in his book *Understanding virtue ethics* (2014) tried to compare virtue ethics and ethics of duty and came to the conclusion that "Virtue ethics does a better job at performing the four tasks of moral theory: to understand morality, to prescribe norms, to justify them and to describe how they fit into our lives" (p. 48). He claimed that "there is no uncontentious, objective, metaphysical or a priori foundation" to build an ethics of duty, but that "character as shaped by community or tradition can motivate such a critique because of its inherent creativity and sensitiv-ity to value" (p. 41).

As we see from this analysis there are no reasons to keep virtue ethics as a separate body of contemporary philosophy. It should be conceptually embedded into normative, positive, and practical ethics to achieve a more efficient theoretical framework. As a separate discipline it should be studied only in history of ethics.

REFERENCES

Anscombe, Gertrude Elizabeth Margaret. 1958. Modern Moral Philosophy. *Philosophy* 33 (124): 1–19.
Audi, Robert. 2004. *The Good in the Right: A Theory of Intuition and Intrinsic Value*. Princeton University Press.
Ayer, A.J. 1936. *Language, Truth and Logic*. Courier Corporation.
Blackburn, Simon. 1993. *Essays in Quasi-Realism*. Oxford University Press on Demand.
———. 2006. Antirealist Expressivism and Quasi-Realism. In *The Oxford Handbook of Ethical Theory*, ed. David Copp, 146–162. Oxford University Press.
Brewer, Kathryn Balstad. 1997. Management as a Practice: A Response to Alasdair MacIntyre. *Journal of Business Ethics* 16 (8): 825–833.
Devettere, Raymond J. 2002. *Introduction to Virtue Ethics: Insights of the Ancient Greeks*. Georgetown University Press.
Forsyth, Donelson R. 1992. Judging the Morality of Business Practices: The Influence of Personal Moral Philosophies. *Journal of Business Ethics* 11 (5): 461–470.
Hare, Richard Mervyn. 1952. *The Language of Morals*. Oxford Paperbacks.
Harman, Gilbert. 1977. *The Nature of Morality: An Introduction to Ethics*. Oxford University Press.
Hernandez, Jill Graper, ed. 2011. *The New Intuitionism*. Bloomsbury Publishing.
Huemer, Michael. 2005. *Ethical Intuitionism*. Palgrave Macmillan.
Limbs, Eric C., and Timothy L. Fort. 2000. Nigerian Business Practices and Their Interface with Virtue Ethics. *Journal of Business Ethics* 26 (2): 169–179.
MacIntyre, Alasdair. 1985. *After Virtue*. London: Duckworth.
Nowell-Smith, Patrick Horace. 1954. *Ethics*. London: Penguin Books.
Oakley, Justin, and Dean Cocking. 2001. *Virtue Ethics and Professional Roles*. Cambridge University Press.
Prichard, Harold Arthur. 1912. Does Moral Philosophy Rest on a Mistake? *Mind* 21 (81): 21–37.
Ross, William D. 1930. *The Right and the Good*. Oxford: Clarendon Press.
Sadler-Smith, Eugene. 2012. Before Virtue: Biology, Brain, Behavior, and the "Moral Sense". *Business Ethics Quarterly* 22 (2): 351–376.
Sayre-McCord, Geoffrey. 1996. Coherentist Epistemology and Moral Theory. In *Moral Knowledge: New Readings*, ed. Walter Sinnott-Armstrong and Mark Timmons. Oxford University Press.

Sinnott-Armstrong, Walter. 2006. Moral Intuitionism Meets Empirical Psychology. In *Metaethics After Moore*, ed. T. Horgan and M. Timmons, 339–365. Oxford University Press on Demand.

———. 2011. An Empirical Challenge to Moral Intuitionism. In *The New Intuitionism*, ed. Jill Graper Hernandez, 11–28. London: Continuum.

Sison, Alejo José G., Edwin M. Hartman, and Joan Fontrodona. 2012. Guest Editors' Introduction Reviving Tradition: Virtue and the Common Good in Business and Management. *Business Ethics Quarterly* 22 (2): 207–210.

Solomon, Robert C. 1992. Corporate Roles, Personal Virtues: An Aristotelean Approach to Business Ethics. *Business Ethics Quarterly* 2 (3): 317–339.

Stevenson, Charles Leslie. 1937. The Emotive Meaning of Ethical Terms. *Mind* 46 (181): 14–31.

———. 1944. *Ethics and Language*. New Haven, CT: Yale University Press.

Stocker, Michael. 1976. The Schizophrenia of Modern Ethical Theories. *The Journal of Philosophy* 73 (14): 453–466.

Swanton, C. 2003. *Virtue Ethics: A Pluralistic View*. NewYork: Oxford University Press.

Timmons, Mark. 1999. *Morality Without Foundations: A Defense of Ethical Contextualism*. Oxford University Press on Demand.

Van Hooft, Stan. 2014. *Understanding Virtue Ethics*. Routledge.

Index[1]

[1]Note: Page numbers followed by 'n' refer to notes.

© The Author(s) 2018
M. Storchevoy, *A Scientific Approach to Ethics*,
https://doi.org/10.1007/978-3-319-69113-8

143

Printed by Books on Demand, Germany